HISTORIC
SCHENECTADY
COUNTY
A Bicentennial History

by Bill Buell

Uncle John,

Enjoy the book!

Bill Buell

Commissioned by the Schenectady County Historical Society

Historical Publishing Network
A division of Lammert Incorporated
San Antonio, Texas

ACKNOWLEDGEMENTS

The author would like to thank the Schenectady County Historical Society President Ed Reilly, Librarian Katherine Chansky and Curator Kathryn Weller for their help in putting together this book, as well as past presidents Frank Taormina and Kim Mabee. Also making the job much easier was a wonderful group of volunteers at the society, including Cindy Seacord and Carol Lewis, as well as 2008 summer intern Mandi Beecroft, whose help collecting photos was indispensable. Also, special thanks to my wife Sarah for helping me stay focused on the project.

All photographs and images are from the collections of the Schenectady County Historical Society, the *Daily Gazette*, and the U.S. Library of Congress, as well as the personal collections of Noel Reidinger-Johnson and Jeff Haraden.

First Edition

Copyright © 2009 Historical Publishing Network

ISBN: 9781935377078
Library of Congress Card Catalog Number: 2009935099

Historic Schenectady County: A Bicentennial History

author:	Bill Buell
editor:	Ed Reilly
cover artist:	L. F. Tantillo
contributing writers for "Sharing the Heritage":	Pam Sustar
	Joe Goodpasture

Historical Publishing Network

president:	Ron Lammert
project manager:	Barry Black
administration:	Donna M. Mata
	Melissa G. Quinn
	Evelyn Hart
book sales:	Dee Steidle
production:	Colin Hart
	Glenda Tarazon Krouse
	Craig Mitchell
	Charles A. Newton, III
	Roy Arellano

CONTENTS

INTRODUCTION

After extensive research and careful deliberation, Peter Stephen Du Ponceau had it all figured out. A French-born American lawyer, Du Ponceau had a command of many different European languages and was also an expert on Indian dialects. In an 1822 letter to George W. Featherstonhaugh, Du Ponceau explained that the name the Dutch picked for the small village they settled on the Mohawk River in upstate New York back in the 1660s was probably Sgachnectatich.

"It is, in my opinion, entirely Indian without any addition from the Dutch language," Du Ponceau wrote to Featherstonhaugh. He went on to add that "the English, you know, always drop the guttural ch, which they can not pronounce, therefore they pronounced the word Scanectati, Skanectady or Schenectady. I have no doubt that this is the true and only true etymology of the famous name of your famous town." Du Ponceau surmised that the name's origin was from the Onondaga or Mohawk people, and referred to a "Hollander" or "Dutchman," but the standard meaning most often used today is "beyond the pine plains," or some variation of it. Arendt Van Curler, the settlement's founder, called the area the "Great Flats," the French named it Corlaer, in Van Curler's honor, and to many early settlers it was Schonowe. There were 79 different spellings of Schenectady according to George Roberts, who published "Old Schenectady" in 1905, but amazingly New York Colonial Governor Peter Stuyvesant got it exactly right—at least how it's spelled today—in one of his written orders in 1663.

Regardless of how you spell the name, it is unlike any other in today's world—a statement equally true when applied to area history. Schenectady is one of the smallest counties in New York, yet its story seems unparalleled. At the forefront of the American experience in the two centuries before the county was officially formed in 1809, it has shone with unusual light through much of the two centuries since.

At the time of European settlement, it was the New World's western frontier. It served, in the early part of the 19th century, as the gateway west for thousands of Americans, first by canal boat and then by rail. The Mohawk River and the valley it carved out during the last Ice Age was the way pioneers and settlers made their way into America's interior. But even after modern advances in transportation made Schenectady's geographical position less relevant, the city became a key component in the country's march into the Industrial Age.

While the motto, "the city that lights and hauls the world," might no longer apply, Schenectady, city and county, remains a key player in the Capital Region of upstate New York, serving both as a home to the arts—which has helped revitalize its downtown core—and as a scientific and technological magnet for research in fields such as nanotechnology.

CHAPTER I

THE BEGINNING

ARENDT VAN CURLER

In July of 1667, Arendt Van Curler left Schenectady and headed north to Canada, his mission, as it had been so many times before, to keep peace between the many competing factions living within the northern region of Colonial America. Unfortunately, he never got there. He drowned in Lake Champlain under suspicious circumstances, perhaps at the hands of his trusted Indian allies, the Mohawks.

The unanswered questions surrounding his death are an interesting sidebar to New York history, but more compelling is the story of Van Curler's impact on Schenectady and the colony as a whole during his lifetime.

More than two decades before he founded Schenectady in 1661, Van Curler was a key figure in the development of New Netherland by the Dutch, who first laid claim to the area in 1609 after Henry Hudson sailed up the river that now bears his name for the Dutch East India Company.

Van Curler came over from Nijkerk, Holland, in 1638, fourteen years after Albany, then called Fort Orange, was initially settled, and was as responsible as anyone for the successful colonization of New York. Initially the manager of the huge manor, Rensselaerwyck, Van Curler became the driving force behind the settlement of Schenectady, at the time a frontier outpost on the south banks of the Mohawk

Arendt Van Curler.

ILLUSTRATION BY CARL BUELL.

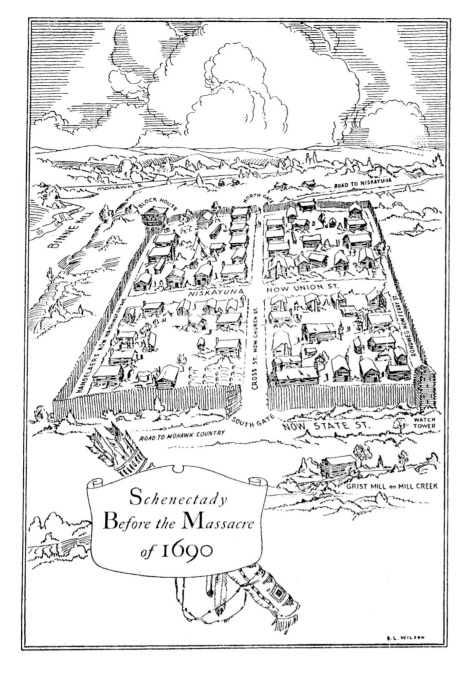

ROAD TO NISKAYUNA

BLOCK HOUSE

NORTH GATE

MOHAWK R.

BINNE

HANNELAERS ON WASHINGTON AVE.

NISKAYUNA

NOW UNION ST.

CROSS ST. NOW CHURCH ST.

RONDWEG NOW FERRY ST.

SOUTH GATE

ROAD TO MOHAWK COUNTRY

NOW STATE ST.

WATCH TOWER

GRIST MILL on MILL CREEK

Schenectady
Before the Massacre
of 1690

B. L. WILSON

❖

For many schoolchildren growing up in Schenectady during the 1940s and 1950s, this was what Schenectady in 1690 looked like. Unfortunately, the image, created for the sesquicentennial celebration in 1940 by Bradley L. Wilson of the General Electric Company, is not historically accurate. The stockade walls most likely did not cover the entire village, and a number of the structures, including the block house, are in the wrong location.

River, about fifteen miles west of where it flows into the Hudson. As fine an example of the Dutch entrepreneurial spirit as anyone, Van Curler believed that commerce worked best free of conflict, and as a result he was constantly brokering peace treaties, not only between the Dutch and their enemies, but also between the French and the English, the French and the Mohawks, the English and the Mohawks, and the Mohawks and their Indian rivals to the east, the Mahicans.

Kiliaen Van Rensselaer, the original proprietor of Rensselaerwyck, never actually set foot in the new world, but instead sent Van Curler, a

nephew and just eighteen years old at the time, to take care of his interests. Van Rensselaer admonished him in one letter, "I hear that you spend too much time in the woods; that ought not to be," and the distant uncle was no doubt dismayed to hear from a local correspondent, Domine Johannes Megapolensis, that Van Curler was "completed addicted" to alcohol. But despite his age and the occasional angry missive from Van Rensselaer, Van Curler seems to have done a pretty good job of dealing with most of the challenges presented him.

If Van Curler did drink as much as the Domine suggests, it doesn't seem to have affected his dealings with others, and as for his walks into the woods, those forays into Indian territory helped secure the region for the Dutch and kept things relatively peaceful in the Mohawk Valley. It was during one of those western excursions, in September of 1642, that Van Curler first got a good look at the area of land that would become Schenectady. On his way back from a Mohawk village at Auriesville after failing to secure the release of a French priest, Van Curler was so impressed by what he saw from an open ridge somewhere in the West Glenville hills, he wrote to Van Rensselaer; "Hardly half a day's journey from the Colonie there lies the most beautiful land on the Maquas Kill that ever eye saw, full a day's journey long and mostly in one unbroken piece. It is impossible to reach it by boat, on account of the strong current which prevails there; and on the other hand, on account of the shallowness of the water, but I think it may be possible to reach it by wagon."

It wasn't until 1661 that Van Curler—he was now in his early forties—decided to move to that "most beautiful land." His two decades of fair dealings with the Indians had put him in their good favor, and later that year he purchased the land from the Mohawks for "six hundred hands of good Wheyte Wampum, six Koates of Duffels, thirty barrs of Lead, and nine bags of gunpowder." That made the Indians happy, but while six to eight families began taking possession of the land, authorities in Albany and governor Peter Stuyvesant put restrictions on the settlers, allowing them only to farm. Those who took part in the fur trade would be arrested.

There were twelve others who, along with Van Curler, became the original proprietors of

Schenectady, including Alexander Lindsay Glen, a Scot who had settled on the north side of the river a few years earlier, in 1658, in what is now Scotia.

Van Curler built his home at the northwest corner of North Church and Union Streets, and went about the business of building a community. In large part that meant his duties as peacekeeper and negotiator would continue. In 1667 his skills as a mediator necessitated a trip to Canada, but unfortunately he never got there.

While Van Curler may have worked hard and successfully to keep the Indians peaceful in New Netherland, there was little he could do to stop the Mohawks and their raiding parties from heading north to Canada. In revenge the French and their Indian allies traveled into the Mohawk Valley in the winter of 1666 to attack Iroquois villages. Ill-equipped and suffering from poor planning, the raiders lost their way in the snow not far from Schenectady and became trapped by the Mohawks, who killed 11 soldiers and wounded several others. On the verge of annihilation, the French were saved by Van Curler, who convinced the Mohawks to return to their villages to guard against the possibility of a larger French force on its way. When the Mohawks left, French soldiers straggled into Schenectady and Van Curler took care of them, offering food to the starving and sending the wounded on to Albany.

The English took over control of New Netherland when its fleet sailed into New York harbor in 1664 and Governor Peter Stuyvesant —with no one willing to help—was forced to meekly relinquish power to a new English governor, Richard Nichols. In 1667 the viceroy in New France, Seigneur de Tracy, perhaps spurred by Van Curler's kindness to French troops a year earlier, offered an invitation to the Dutchman to visit Canada.

Joined by two Dutchmen, a German, a Frenchman he had rescued from the Indians, and five Mohawks, including a woman and a child, Van Curler began heading North in mid-summer. But the weather turned violent as his party was crossing Lake Champlain, causing the canoe to capsize. All five European men and the child drowned; only the Mohawks and their woman survived. At the inquest following his

death, the Mohawks said that Van Curler, against their wishes, would not turn around and paddle with the wind, refused to throw the provisions overboard, and failed to strip as they did, making it much harder to swim or stay afloat. The Indians also said that Van Curler had earlier failed to show the proper respect at a Mohawk holy site on the lake and that was the reason he died.

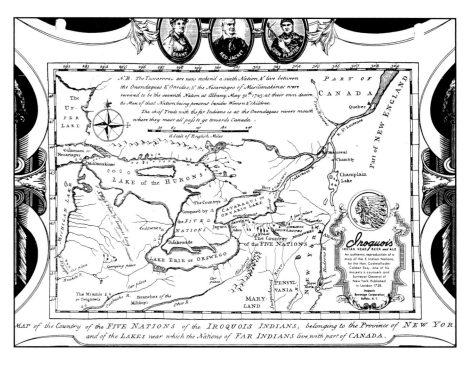

MAP of the Country of the FIVE NATIONS of the IROQUOIS INDIANS, belonging to the Province of NEW YOR and of the LAKES near which the Nations of FAR INDIANS live, with part of CANADA.

Some historians have suggested that the Mohawks' story is less than credible. Could Van Curler, a man who typically made the right decision in nearly thirty years in the New World, had made so many wrong moves on this one occasion? Instead, is it possible that Van Curler, while still loved and revered by most Mohawks, fell in with a bunch who harbored some resentment toward him because of the many times he had stopped them from spilling French blood? Barring unforeseen new evidence about Van Curler's death, it's a question that will never be answered.

What is more certain is Van Curler's positive impact on New York history. Despite the assertions of Donna Merwick in her 1990 book, *Possessing Albany: 1630-1710: The Dutch and English Experiences*, which suggests Van Curler's contribution was overstated by historians of the 18th and 19th centuries, Van Curler's value to the new colony seems clear. In

A map of New York, first published in 1728, indicates where the Indian nations lived, and features three of the Iroquois' greatest leaders, Joseph Brandt, Red Jacket, and Corn Planter.

❖

Above: This Giles F. Yates sketch of the Schenectady Massacre is from Pearson's 1883 book, The History of the Schenectady Patent.

Below: Before he lived at Fort Johnson and Johnson Hall, William Johnson called Schenectady home.

her 1975 book, *Stubborn for Liberty: The Dutch in New York*, Alice P. Kenney puts Van Curler on the same level as William Johnson and Peter Schuyler for his ability to deal with Indians. In two more recent works, Susan J. Staffa's *Schenectady Genesis: How a Dutch Colonial Village Became an American City, ca. 1661-1800*, and James W. Bradley's *Before Albany: An Archaeology of Native-Dutch Relations in the Capital Region, 1600-1664*, both authors seem to support Kenney's assessment of Van Curler, not Merwick's. Staffa concluded that Van Curler was "a man of vision, grit and determination who exhibited special genius in dealing with crises of cultural confrontation," and that "No man enjoyed more rapport with [the Indians] than he." Bradley, meanwhile, wrote "It was Van Curler's attitude toward native people that made him so different from many of his predecessors and contemporaries. Unlike [Hans Jorisz] Hontom or [Willem] Kieft, Van Curler treated native people as intelligent adults instead of wayward children."

THE MASSACRE

The casualty list for the French and Indian attackers following the Schenectady Massacre of 1690 was minimal: two dead and one seriously wounded. There's nothing in the official record about just how those casualties were received, but if you believe local legend—and in this case there seems little reason not to—those French losses probably came at the hands of defender Adam Vrooman.

Near midnight on February 8, a Saturday, 114 Frenchmen, 80 "Praying" Mohawks (those who had earlier been converted to Catholicism by the French) and 16 Algonquins attacked the sleepy village of Schenectady through the north gate, near Vrooman's house, and for two hours terrorized the citizens, killing 60—including 10 women and 12 children—and taking 27 captive. Vrooman's story, passed on from

generation to generation, tells of the staunch resistance he offered at his home, and how the Indians were so impressed by his defense that they eventually left his property and moved elsewhere. Unfortunately, Vrooman's wife Engeltje Bloom Ryckman and their baby daughter, the youngest of six children, were killed while making a dash for safety. Vrooman also lost his father, Hendrick, and a brother, Bartholomew, in the attack, and according to *The Vrooman Family in New York*, two of Adam's sons, Barent and Wouter, were among the 27 captured. Both were later released and returned to Schenectady.

The Schenectady Massacre is a classic American story and a perfect example of just how badly things can go wrong when the amalgamation of world and local politics forces itself on a small community. Van Curler's town had between 250 and 300 people living there in 1690, and while there was always a concern about Indian attack, Schenectadians' friendly relations with the local Mohawks kept those concerns at a minimum.

The Glorious Revolution of 1689 changed the ruling party in England, and for many in the New World that meant that a change in the colonies was also in order. Those in charge in New York, however, weren't ready to relinquish that power, and as a result Schenectady was a divided community on February 8, 1690.

Vrooman received a letter from the new leader in New York City, Jacob Leisler, asking him to become the crown's new representative in Schenectady. A friend of Johannes Glen, the constable at the time, Vrooman declined the offer. There were others, however, who hoped to see the Glens relinquish their power and to take their place. The apocryphal stories of Johannes Glen being chased back across the Mohawk to the safety of his home in Scotia the night before the massacre, or the tale of snowmen guarding the gates may or may not be true. The point is that Schenectady was not a unified community in February of 1690, and it paid dearly because of it. Even a detachment of 24 soldiers from Connecticut couldn't stop the French and their Indians from avenging an earlier attack by the Mohawks on the Canadian town of Lacine. Symon Schermerhorn jumped on his horse and rode to Albany to warn the community there,

but by the end of their work in Schenectady that night the French and Indians had only one thought; to return home. They paid a visit to the Glen home the next morning but because of previous kindnesses by that family toward the French and Indians, there were no hostilities. Glen was actually allowed to save some of the captives from a horrible trip north by telling the Indians they were his relatives. He reputedly selected as many people as he could before the Indians began questioning the size of his extended family.

After Schermerhorn sounded the alarm to Albany, a group of Mohawks, led by a warrior who went by the Christian name of Lawrence, joined forces with some Mahicans and chased the invaders back to Canada, killing 16 Frenchmen and three Indians along the way.

A TOWN REBUILDS

Following the massacre, the freshly widowed Adam Vrooman quickly remarried in 1691, and again in 1697 after his second wife died. His sawmills made him one of the town's most prosperous citizens, but in 1711 he left Schenectady and bought land in Schoharie County, and moved there in 1723 before his death in 1730, by most accounts at the age of eighty-one.

Schenectady itself also rebounded. Although the town and its surrounding area was drastically depopulated immediately following the attack in 1690, its prime location insured its survival. Situated west of Albany at a point where the Mohawk River was somewhat navigable, Schenectady was the gateway west and as a result became a prominent ship-building community. It was, however, still made to feel as if it was little more than an appendage to Albany, officials there having control of the fur trade and still harshly restricting Schenectady's desire to deal commercially with the Indians. The only exception to this rule had been back in 1672 when Van Curler's widow, Antonia Slaghboom, had been granted a license by Albany to trade with the Indians. Not only had Antonia lost her husband a few years earlier, but much of her property as well due to a fire. She was evidently a sympathetic-enough figure that the hierarchy in Albany agreed she should have special privileges.

They didn't feel so compassionate about the rest of the population in Schenectady, however, and, by 1723, Johannes Mynderse had had enough. A dram shop operator who had carried on illegal trade with the Mohawks for years, Mynderse was clearly in violation of the law and was arrested. On this occasion, however, Mynderse refused to pay the fine and was jailed

Survivors of the Beukendaal Massacre in July of 1748 took refuge in the DeGraff House.

by the magistrate in Albany. He eventually received a writ of habeas corpus that got him out of jail, and then commenced to sue the Albany Common Council for trespass and false imprisonment. Albany's leaders didn't seem particularly concerned by Mynderse's suit, proclaiming their hopes that "an ordinance be made for the better regulation of the Indian trade in Albany, against Schenectady and elsewhere to the westward, northward and eastward."

To everyone's surprise but particularly Albany's, the colony's royal court decided in favor of Mynderse in 1727, thereby bringing an end to Albany's monopoly of the fur trade. Schenectady, after more than sixty years of subservience to Albany, had become its own master.

THE BEUKENDAAL MASSACRE

To the people of Schenectady and the surrounding area, the Mohawk River was more than just a source of water or a way west. In the 17th and 18th centuries, it was, primarily, a security blanket, and the closer you were to it, preferably on its southern banks, the safer you were. But as more people followed the dream of working their own land, farms started popping up throughout the Mohawk Valley, and getting a choice spread right on the river was impossible for many.

Jan Mabee's farm, now a historical site and property of the Schenectady County Historical Society, is reputedly the oldest house built in the Mohawk Valley and by all accounts never came under Indian attack. It was built on the southern side of the river just a few miles west of Schenectady in the late seventeenth century, and by the 1740s it was no longer the western frontier, having been supplanted by the Palatine settlements in Schoharie County in the early 1720s, a trading post in Oswego in 1727, and in 1740 by William Johnson's stone house on the

northern bank of the Mohawk just west of present-day Amsterdam. Between Johnson's presence and the continued good relations with the Mohawks, those living in Schenectady and the surrounding areas probably felt pretty safe and secure. The horrors of the Schenectady Massacre fifty-four years earlier must have seemed awfully distant, but in the early spring of 1744 life in the colony once again turned perilous.

Following King William's War (1689-1697) and Queen Anne's War (1702-1713), yet another confrontation, King George's War, came to New York when King Louis XV of France declared war on England's King George II.

In November of 1745 the French and Indians attacked the community in Saratoga (now Schuylerville), 30 miles northeast of Schenectady, killing 30 people and taking 60 captives. During a particularly bloody four-month stretch in the summer of 1746 the Schenectady and Albany area was subjected to 30 different raids by their enemies from the north. In May, Symon Groot's farm, just west of the Mabee house, was attacked and Symon and two of his brothers were killed. More than 100 men set out from Schenectady and chased the raiders back toward Canada but failed to engage them, and later that year in October, Abraham DeGraff and his son William were both taken captive from their farm in Scotia. The elder DeGraff died in Quebec on June 12, 1747.

A year later, on July 19, 1748, tragedy again hit the Schenectady community in a big way.

Daniel Toll, a neighbor of DeGraff, was out trying to round up stray horses with the help of Dirk Van Vorst and a slave when they stumbled upon a French and Indian encampment. In an exchange of musket fire, Toll was killed but Van Vorst and the slave escaped. Another farmer in the area, Adrian Van Slyck, heard the gunfire and sent his slave to Schenectady for help. A group of sixty volunteers, eager to exact revenge on the French and Indians for their dealings with the Groots and DeGraffs, did not wait for the militia to be called out and raced to the area looking for a fight.

What they saw when they got there was Toll tied to a tree, looking as if he was waving for help. It was a trap, with Toll's body placed there to lure rescuers. That first band of 60 was closely followed by small groups of other men,

❖

A historical marker indicates the site of the Beukendaal Massacre just east of the Village of Scotia. The sign was erected by the Schenectady Chapter of the Daughters of the American Revolution.

including one led by Jacob Glen, but the French and Indians were more organized and better fighters on this day. In vicious hand-to-hand combat, much of it around the deserted DeGraff farmhouse, 20 Schenectady men were killed and 13 more captured. What became known as the Beukendaal Massacre left the Schenectady community in a state of grief that must have rivaled the aftermath of the 1690 massacre. Among the dead were family members of the Glens, Vroomans, Bradts, Van Slycks, and Van Antwerps.

JOHNSON FIGHTS THE FRENCH

By 1740 most people in Schenectady had probably heard of William Johnson, an enterprising young Irishmen who had two years earlier built a house just west of present-day Amsterdam on the Mohawk River. By the end of the decade, Johnson was the most influential

man in the Mohawk Valley and was rapidly becoming, arguably the most significant person in the history of Colonial America.

Throughout King George's War, while many New Yorkers moved back East to the safety of Schenectady, Johnson remained at his home 18 miles further west on the river, confident "the Mohawks will defend me." He did, however, send his common-law wife Catty and their three children back to Schenectady in 1748 because of the danger.

The period following King George's War saw the population of the Mohawk Valley, including the Schoharie watershed, nearly double to around five thousand people, but the respite from war was short-lived. On August 24, 1754, before official hostilities had actually begun and a year before the defeat of British General Braddock in western Pennsylvania, the French and Indian War, or Seven Years War as it was called in Europe, came to upstate New York: Hoosick, a settlement east of Albany, was attacked by

The Mabee Farm, which dates back to the turn of the 17th century, was one of the first houses built west of Schenectady. It is owned by the Schenectady County Historical Society.

Indians. Schenectady prepared for the worst by renovating Queen's Fort, the blockhouse that had been built in 1735, but as serious as the threat was, the village never again actually came under physical attack. It was, however, a hotbed of activity throughout the war, serving as a point of departure for various British and Colonial troops.

Johnson, who had been appointed the commander of the Albany militia back in 1748, was again in command of the local militias. Serving under him and commissioned as officers were men like Daniel Campbell and John Sanders. Campbell was a Scotsman who had

arrived in Schenectady in 1754 and become close friends with Johnson, while Sanders was an Albany native who had married Deborah Glen, the great-grand-daughter of Alexander Lindsay Glen, and taken up residence in his wife's Scotia mansion. Five Schenectady militia companies served under Johnson, and military victories in September of 1755 at Lake George and July of 1759 at Niagara made Johnson an American hero. The success at Niagara began in June on the flats west of Scotia as 4,000 British troops and 2,200 colonials camped together on their way west. It was the largest military encampment ever seen in the Mohawk Valley.

Another individual who would make a name for himself during the French and Indian War was Christopher Yates. Commissioned a captain at the age of 23, Yates was the son of Joseph Yates, Jr., who had a large farm just north of Schenectady, and the nephew of Abraham Yates, Jr., an Albany politician who would become one of the most powerful figures there during the American Revolution. The younger Yates' contributions at Niagara didn't go unnoticed by Johnson, and the two men became close friends. Most of the fighting in the French and Indian War was over by September of 1760, and the official end came with the treaty of Paris in February of 1763.

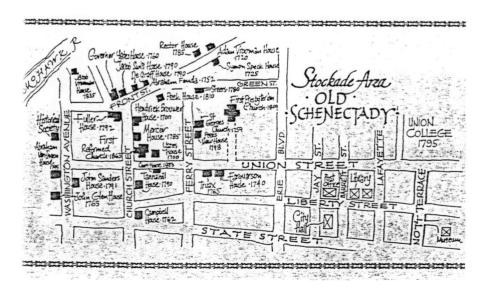

CHAPTER II

THE AMERICAN REVOLUTION

BATTLE OF NORMANSKILL

The summer of 1777 was not an easy time for Schenectadians interested in breaking with the mother country. The British were coming, seemingly from all directions; local Tories were feeling quite smug about their prospects; Daniel Campbell and John Sanders, two prominent citizens, were refusing to deal with continental currency; and Christopher Yates, the man most Schenectadians looked to for guidance in these troubled times, was out of town, engaged elsewhere in patriotic pursuits.

It was a time when nerves were so frayed that the Schenectady Committee of Correspondence, officially a sub-committee of the Albany group, was meeting on a regular basis, sometimes even twice a day. August 11th was one of those days. Chairman Ryneer Mynderse, having put the militia and a small group of Continental troops from Rhode Island on full alert a day earlier and having overseen a morning session to discuss some issues regarding local slaves and their own designs on independence, called together the Committee of Correspondence again at 3 p.m. With information received earlier that day from Jacob Schermerhorn, Mynderse revealed that a large group of his fellow citizens, those still loyal to the crown, were congregating at Nicholas Van Patten's farm on the Normanskill looking to make trouble. With Yates away near Fort Edward trying to slow down British

This sketch reputedly drawn in 1783 by a tutor of the Yates children, shows Christopher Yates in his home at 26 Front Street, surrounded by four of his sons and three of their cousins.

Above: Normanskill marker.

Below: William Johnson.

General Johnny Burgoyne and his troops as they marched southward, it was left for someone else to heed the call to action.

In the hours of darkness on the 11th and 12th, the Schenectady militia under Major Abraham Swits and a force of the Continental troops under Captain Childs, marching on Mynderse's orders, swooped down on the Tories in Van Patten's barn and routed them. One individual, a well-known loyalist named David Springer, was killed, 13 more were taken captive, and the rest, numbering around 100, were dispersed. The combined force of the Continental troops and local militia was also around 100, and while the confrontation took place in what is now Albany County, this was definitely Schenectady's fight, and its citizens were rightfully proud of producing what was seen as a huge psychological victory for the American side.

It was the beginning of a reversal in fortune for the Patriots, who earlier that summer had learned of the abandonment of Fort Ticonderoga on July 6, a defeat at Hubbardton, Vermont, on July 7, St. Leger's siege of Fort Stanwix, which began on August 2, and the Battle of Oriskany on August 6. At Oriskany, American troops were routed and General Nicholas Herkimer was mortally wounded, creating a pall over upstate New York that left Patriots in despair and Loyalists emboldened. The "Battle of Normanskill" began to change all that.

Less than a week after the events on the Normanskill, the American side won a huge

victory at the Battle of Bennington. The siege of Fort Stanwix ended on August 22 as St. Leger, deserted by many of his Indian allies, packed up and headed back to the safety of Oswego, and before the month was over the British advance up the Hudson was checked at Kingston. On September 19 the Battle of Bemis Heights, and on October 7 the Battle of Freeman's Farm—the two engagements making up the Battles of Saratoga—added greatly to the American success. On October 17, a little more than two months after a force of Patriots from Schenectady had squelched a Tory uprising at the Van Patten farm, Burgoyne surrendered at Saratoga and the American cause of independence for the first time seemed like a real possibility.

THE COMMITTEE OF CORRESPONDENCE

Schenectady held its first committee of correspondence meeting on May 6, 1775, nearly a year after William Johnson's death in July of 1774 and just a few short weeks after "the shot heard round the world" in Lexington, Massachusetts, had officially marked the beginning of the American Revolution. Johnson's passing certainly lessened the crown's influence in New York, and on January 24, 1775, four months before the Schenectady group formed, Albany held the initial committee of correspondence meeting, with several Schenectady residents in attendance. At that meeting, Abraham Yates, Jr., a man with no official ties to England and certainly not a member of New York's elite class (such as the Schuylers, Van Rensselaers, and the Livingstons, to name a few), was unanimously selected as chairman, and a new governing body overseeing upstate New York affairs was born.

Schenectady was one of several districts—others included Halfmoon, Saratoga, Ballston, and Schaghticoke—that had been created in the present-day counties of Albany, Schenectady, Rensselaer, Saratoga, Washington, Columbia, Greene, and Schoharie, to handle governing decisions that had previously been the charge of the crown and its representatives. At the May 6 meeting in Schenectady, Christopher Yates, Abraham's nephew, was named chairman of the

Schenectady subcommittee, and the very first topic of discussion—after Yates' election—was what to do with Daniel Campbell and the large quantity of gunpowder he had at his disposal.

A good friend of Johnson's, Campbell was a Scotsman who had come to Schenectady twenty years earlier and made plenty of money in the Indian trade. He had also served during the French and Indian War, but having amassed great wealth under British rule, he was in no hurry to put his fortune at risk. It was determined by the Schenectady committee that they would purchase Campbell's gunpowder from him and make it available to citizen patriots, thus ensuring that it would not get into British hands. It was only the beginning of a series of confrontations between Campbell and the committee that would last for much of the war. But while Campbell and Sanders maneuvered to maintain some measure of neutrality, some Schenectadians were pronounced loyalists. "Schoolmaster Fletcher," for instance, warned that John Johnson and his Indian allies would swarm down the Mohawk River and cut off Schenectady from the rest of the colony, and that if he had it in his power, he "would do the same, for you are all rebels."

Joseph Kingsley, meanwhile, was another Schenectadian who on two occasions was arrested for making known his loyalist leanings. Kingsley denied the charge of actually working against the Patriot cause to the men of the Schenectady Committee, but he did concede that his sentiments in regard to the present dispute between Great Britain and the Colonies differed from theirs. Deemed an "offender to the American cause," Kingsley was sent to Albany in February of 1776 for a short stay in jail, and was headed there again a few months later before agreeing to pay a fine for his infraction of speaking out.

As for Campbell and Sanders, these two prominent citizens of Schenectady spent much of the American Revolution trying not to offend either side. The Schenectady Committee did allow Campbell and a friend to visit Montreal on personal business in August of 1775 with the following stipulation: "They have pledged their honor to us that they will not carry any letters or messages of news to or from any person who is enemycal to the American cause." In April of 1776, Campbell made another request for a pass to Canada but this time both the committee and General Philip Schuyler refused him, and by May of 1777 he was considered "dangerous'" by the committee, and targeted for arrest. After a short stay in Albany, Campbell and eight other Schenectadians were paroled and then asked to sign an oath saying they would "not by words or deeds give any counsel, advice or direct aid or comfort to any enemies of the United States of America…."

Campbell signed the paper, but his differences with the committee didn't end there. In July of 1777, when anxiety over the war was at its peak, both Campbell and Sanders were summoned before the committee to explain why they wouldn't accept mortgage payments in Continental currency. The committee initially acted harshly against Sanders, banishing him to jail in Kingston. Before he was sent there, however, the committee postponed the matter, and when Sanders appeared before them again on August 24 and agreed to accept payment in Continental currency, he was free to go.

Sanders, who had also refused to serve on the Committee of Correspondence when it was originally formed, seems to have changed his allegiances at some point soon after the summer of 1777. He helped finance Benjamin Franklin's trip to France, and by 1780 his name was on the rolls of the Albany County Militia. Sanders ended the war as commander of the guard in Schenectady.

Campbell, meanwhile, wasn't so quick to change. In May of 1778 he again had a date with the Committee of Correspondence for "speaking words that in the opinion of the board might have a dangerous tendency and prove detrimental to the liberties of America." In July he refused to take the Oath of Allegiance and was told to ready himself to be "removed within the enemy lines." After getting a temporary suspension of that order, Campbell declared on August 1 that he was ready to take the oath. It didn't happen until May of 1779, but finally Campbell was on the American side and soon after his name also appeared on the muster rolls of the Albany County Militia. While Campbell and Sanders were adept at straddling the fence for much of the war, what made their situation a little more tenable is the prominent standing in

Above: Albany's Philip Schuyler was in charge of the Colonial Army's Northern Department before being relieved of duty during the summer of 1777.

Below: Mohawk warrior, Joseph Brandt, an ally of the Colonists during the French and Indian War, fought alongside the British during the American Revolution.

Above: The Campbell House on the corner of South Church Street and State Street was built sometime between the French and Indian War and the American Revolution.

Bottom, left: Daniel Campbell tried to remain neutral throughout the American Revolution but eventually sided with the Colonists.

Bottom, right: Engeltie Bradt, a descendent of one of Schenectady's thirteen founders, married Daniel Campbell.

the community enjoyed by their wives. Sanders came from Albany and married Deborah Glen, the great-granddaughter of Alexander Lindsay Glen, and Campbell's wife was Engeltie Bradt, the daughter of Arendt Bradt, a tavern owner in Schenectady and a descendant of one of the original fourteen founders. The presence of both women must have tempered the stance taken by the committee against their husbands, and we must assume that both men were in turn greatly influenced by their wives, who had much deeper roots in Schenectady, with various

family members staunchly in support of the American cause.

CHRISTOPHER YATES

The Campbell and Sanders families weren't the only ones in Schenectady dealing with tough issues. Christopher Yates, Schenectady's leading patriot, was not only a good friend of the Johnson family but was also the brother-in-law of John Butler, whose wife was the sister of Yates' wife Jannetje Bradt. Butler and his son,

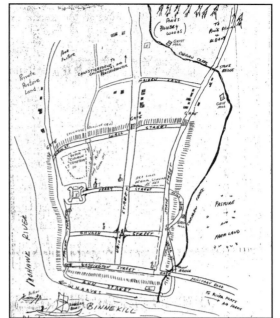

Walter, were loyalists and the leaders of several Tory raids into the Mohawk and Schoharie Valleys throughout the war. The Butler name and that of their close companion Joseph Brandt, a Mohawk warrior, became hated and feared by all Schenectady patriots, and Yates, while evidently never coming face-to-face with his in-laws during the struggle, was constantly on the lookout for them.

Yates resigned from the Committee of Correspondence to take a more active role in the war, and in January of 1776 was commissioned a lieutenant colonel in the Schenectady militia. He was a key figure in General Schuyler's negotiations with the Mohawks early in the war, and throughout much of 1776 and '77 was in command of troops at Fort Anne, where during the Saratoga Campaign he was in charge of slowing down Burgoyne's advance by "felling trees and in otherwise rendering impenetrable the wilderness that lay between Skenesborough [now Whitehall] and Fort Edward." Yates is also credited with helping Polish general and engineer Thaddeus Kosciuszko select the site for the American encampment at Bemis Heights where the first Battle of Saratoga was fought in September of 1777, and the following summer he spent much of his time in the Schoharie Valley trying to defend that area against the

work of the Butlers and their Indian allies. In May of 1779, Yates and the Schenectady militia helped ready the Sullivan and Clinton campaigns for their summer-long attack on the Iroquois by carrying supplies up the Mohawk River, and that service led to Yates being named deputy quartermaster for the Northern Department of the Continental Army for the remainder of the Revolution.

Yates died at the age of forty-eight in 1785, his early passing in part due to wounds

Top, left: An image of Christopher Yates by an unknown artist.

Top, right: A map of Schenectady as it looked at the time of the American Revolution.

Below: Gilbert Stuart's portrait of George Washington.

❖

Money raised by Schenectadians
helped send Benjamin Franklin to
Paris in 1777.

received during the French and Indian War. Along with his wife he left twelve children. One son, Joseph, grew up to become governor of New York, the only Schenectadian to earn that distinction.

When British General Cornwallis surrendered to General Washington at Yorktown in October of 1781 the war was basically over. But the Battle of Johnstown two weeks later and the continuing threat of Tory raids helped keep New York on alert until September of 1783 when the official peace treaty was signed in Paris. Earlier, in June of 1782, Washington visited Schenectady accompanied by Schuyler, and was feted with a public dinner at a tavern owned by Robert Clench. The visit also included a stop at John Sanders' residence for some tea.

CHAPTER III

THE COUNTY'S FIVE TOWNS

DUANESBURG

James Duane had big plans for Duanesburg. A former New York City mayor and a delegate to the first Provincial Congress, Duane was hoping to see his community, about fifteen miles west of the city of Schenectady, blossom into the capital of New York state. As it turned out, Duane died in 1797, while hanging curtains at his house in Schenectady, and his big dreams for Duanesburg never materialized.

His town, however, became the biggest of the five comprising Schenectady County, and along with Niskayuna and Princetown were the three towns making up the county when it was formed in 1809, both Glenville and Rotterdam coming along in 1820 after previously being part of the city.

Located in the western part of the county, Duanesburg was initially given a patent in 1765 as a township, and was first recognized as a town in 1788. With the Mohawk River its northern boundary and the Schoharie Creek on the west, Duanesburg today encompasses about forty-two thousand acres, and includes the small communities of Duanesburg Four Corners, Quaker Street, Delanson, Mariaville, and finally Creekside on the extreme western border.

Born in New York City in 1733, Duane was 3 when his mother died and just 14 at the time of his father's death. He became a ward of wealthy landholder Robert Livingston and moved into Clermont, the Livingston family's Hudson Valley estate.

James Duane hoped to make Duanesburg the capital of New York.

Admitted to the bar in 1754, Duane married Livingston's daughter Maria in 1759, and soon had a busy career as a lawyer, becoming the colony's attorney general in 1767. He initially hoped to see a peaceful resolution to the problems New York and the other 12 colonies were having with Great Britain, and was a proponent of the Galloway Plan, espousing reconciliation with the mother country. Although he regularly served as a delegate to the Continental Congress, Duane missed some time due to ill health and did not sign the Declaration of Independence. He served two terms in the state senate between 1783 and 1790, and was appointed mayor of New York City from 1784-1789. He was also named the first judge of the U.S. District Court in New York by President George Washington in 1789. He served in that capacity until 1794, when continuing health problems forced him to resign.

While most of Duanesburg has maintained its rural and agricultural landscape, the village of Delanson did become a bustling railroad hub during the latter part of the 18th century. Originally called Quaker Street Depot, the small community changed its name to Delanson in 1892 to recognize the impact the Delaware and Hudson Railroad had on the community.

Mariaville was settled in 1792 when Duane decided to build two mills and create a dam, turning a small pond into a lake that he named after his daughter Maria. Duane's daughter Sarah and her husband, George Featherstonhaugh, built a home on Mariaville Lake, while another prominent member of the community was surveyor James Frost. Before he died in 1851, Frost had mapped out much of New York, including the state's northern border with Canada. Frost's son Daniel Marsh Frost, a graduate of West Point, ended up fighting in the Civil War as a brigadier general in the Confederate Army.

PRINCETOWN

The town of Princetown, a long and narrow strip of land to the east of Duanesburg and west of Rotterdam, was created in 1798 and named after John Prince, at the time a state assemblyman from Schenectady. Settling began early in the 18th century by Scots and Irish who had come to the New World and originally made their homes near Ballston Spa and Galway in Saratoga County.

Much of Princetown is situated on hilly terrain, but that didn't stop small communities from springing up in Giffords, Kelly's Station, Rynex Corners, Scotch Church, and Princetown Center. Those areas have remained quite small and today are little more than intersections for the county highway system that runs through the mostly rural town.

In 1853, Princetown Center was home to the Princetown Academy and Female Seminary, a coeducational institution which at one time had as many as 382 students. The grand plan, according to the school's inaugural catalog, was to offer students from Schenectady and the surrounding area an opportunity for education that was "free from all those haunts of vice." The idea seemed like such a good one that many students boarded there, some coming from as far away as Cuba, Scotland, and Germany. The *Schenectady Reflector* heaped praise on the Academy and opined that "a more healthful location can not be found."

Referred to as "truly American and republican," and an "institution of high moral and religious character," Princetown Academy had a strong affiliation with Union College. Many of that school's faculty headed out to Princetown to teach courses at this new school in Elements of Christianity, Greek and Latin Grammar, Rhetoric and Logic, and Analogy of Revealed Religion, to name a few. In 1854 the catalog listed two principals and 10 teachers,

Above: Mary Duane came from one of New York's most prominent families, the Livingstons.

Below: The Beers 1866 Map of Schenectady County.

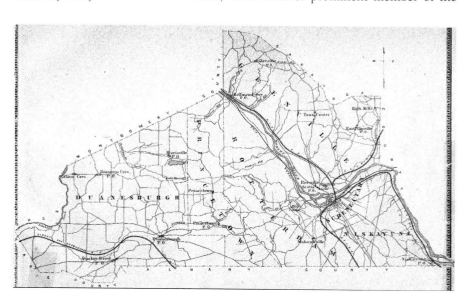

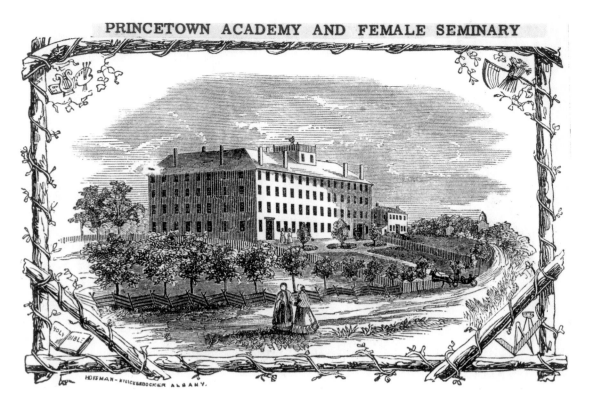

HOFFMAN - KNICKERBOCKER ALBANY.

and the cost per student for a 14-week term was only $28.

Built on land belonging to the Princetown Presbyterian Church, the four-story structure was quite an impressive looking building. The school, however, failed and was closed just three years after it opened. There are very limited contemporary sources explaining why the academy failed, but its demise might have had something to do with low tuition costs and its remote location.

By the time of the American Civil War there was little left of the building. The only remaining evidence on the site is an old well and a historical marker near the intersection of Currybush and Kelly Roads.

Above: The Princetown Academy and Female Seminary, built in 1853, lasted just three years.

Below: The junction of Route 20 and Route 7 in Duanesburg around the turn of the twentieth century.

GLENVILLE

Notwithstanding a close encounter with some friendly fire on the eve of the American Revolution, one big white house on the north bank of the Mohawk River escaped the barbarities of war that were a big part of Colonial New York's history. For more than three quarters of a century, the western frontier in the New World began just west of the Glen Home in Scotia, and during that time, despite its vulnerable geographic location, the building remained a safe haven for all who lived or visited there, be they friend or foe.

River, Glen and his wife Catherine Dongan were on friendly terms with the Iroquois in the area, the Dutch, English, and Germans who followed them to the Mohawk Valley, and the French who, while they made various raids into New York from their home in Canada, never struck a blow at the Glens.

It was Glen's great-granddaughter, Deborah Glen, who nearly became a victim of a wayward tomahawk when two Indians of the Oneida tribe, the only member of the Iroquois Confederacy to side with the Colonials during the American Revolution, got into a confrontation while visiting the house.

❖

Family members pose for the photographer outside the Glen Sanders Mansion in Scotia, c. 1860.

Alexander Lindsay Glen built his first house in what is modern-day Scotia in 1658, three years before Arendt Van Curler began making plans to build his community at Schenectady. A Scotsman who came to America in 1643 and originally settled at Fort Nassau on the Delaware

After their initial argument was broken up, one of the Indians waited behind a door for the other to appear. Upon hearing footsteps heading his way and assuming it was his antagonist, the Indian jumped out from his hiding place and let the tomahawk fly just

as Deborah Glen turned to head up the stairs. The weapon just missed its mark, instead taking a big chunk out of the stairway balustrade.

Along with Scotia and Reesville, a neighboring community that eventually melted into the village of Scotia, the town had hamlets emerge in West Glenville and Alplaus, as well as other smaller settlements in Hoffmans and High Mills. Hoffmans, a few miles west of Scotia, marked the first ferry crossing over the Mohawk River in Glenville, while High Mills was located on the banks of the Alplaus Creek in the northern section of the town.

The town, the only part of Schenectady County located north of the Mohawk River, now encompasses 50.9 square miles, including some of the county's most rugged terrain. Wolf Hollow, a deep gorge in the western part of the town near Hoffmans, was the site of a major Indian battle in 1669 between the Mohawks and the Mahicans. While the two tribes often fought over much of the territory of what is now Schenectady County, this particular confrontation was a decisive victory for the Mohawks and forced the Mahicans to remain east of the Hudson River.

ROTTERDAM

Elias Van Guysling broke the mold. While most of Schenectady's first settlers lived in a small cluster of homes on the south bank of the Mohawk River and then farmed the outlying areas, Van Guysling decided to move out of the safety of the small village in 1670 and build the first house in what is today the town of Rotterdam. Daniel Janse Van Antwerp followed around 1680, and in 1705, on property purchased from Van Antwerp, Jan Pieterse Mabee built a house that still stands today. Mabee's farmhouse, now the Mabee Farm Historic Site, is reputedly the oldest existing structure in the Mohawk Valley.

When Schenectady was incorporated as a city in 1798, Rotterdam was its third ward. It was created as a town in April of 1820, and was made larger in 1853 when it annexed part of the city. There are hamlets today in Pattersonville and Rotterdam Junction, while other small communities such as Mohawkville, Athens Junction, and Van Eppsville are found only in history books. Rotterdam Junction and Athens Junction both played prominent roles in the railroad business during the second half of the 19th century and into the 20th century. The West Shore Railroad, originally the Saratoga and Hudson River Railroad, built a rail yard in 1883-84 that made Rotterdam Junction one of the busiest communities in Schenectady County. The New York Central and Boston and Maine Railroads soon followed, turning Rotterdam Junction into one of the northeast's most popular railroad hubs for nearly half a century. In 1931 things began changing when the Boston and Maine announced that 550 of its workers would be transferred to Mechanicville.

Athens Junction, meanwhile, now that part of Rotterdam's southeast section referred to as Carman, was used by the West Shore largely as a freight bypass. In order to avoid steep grades

A view of the Glen Sanders Mansion in Scotia from across the Mohawk River.

on the main line and to keep freight traffic out of Albany and Schenectady, the West Shore built a line from Castleton to Carman to Hoffmans (just west of Schenectady). The Carman Cut-off, as it was called, opened in 1902.

The name change from Athens Junction to Carman occurred some time around the turn of the century to reflect the influence of William Carman, a former grocer and postmaster whose general store was right at the main railroad crossing.

NISKAYUNA

Alexander Alexander had figured out how to harness water power from the Mohawk River. His next goal was to build a bridge across it.

After securing a permit from the state legislature in 1804 to build a rolling dam on the Mohawk—a dam that deeply enriched his mill business in Niskayuna—Alexander also decided to erect a bridge near that same site that would allow him to more easily tap into the market in Alplaus, a small village on the northern side of the Mohawk, as well as all points north.

In 1805 Alexander's Bridge was built about fifty yards west of the present Rexford Bridge,

and while heavy ice the following spring damaged the structure considerably, that area was generally considered the best place for a crossing. As a result a small community developed there and has been referred to as either Aqueduct or Craig, and sometimes even Alexander's Mills. In some histories Craig more specifically refers to a small cluster of homes up on the hill away from the river.

Aqueduct, where the Erie Canal crossed the river just yards away from where Alexander had built his bridge, is generally what the area is called today, although it never has been an official governmental entity. There was a railroad station built there in 1843 as well as one further east in the hamlet of Niskayuna when the Troy and Schenectady Railroad line was completed.

The Town of Niskayuna wasn't officially formed until March of 1809 when Schenectady County was created, although the area had long been referred to by that name, going as far back as when the Dutch began settling there in the mid-17th century. Throughout the Colonial era and up until 1809 it had been part of the Town of Watervliet in Albany County, and its name is derived from a small band of Native Americans

The Charles Stanford Home on the corner of Balltown Road and Route 5 as it looked in the 1870s.

Opposite, top: Dennison's was a popular general store in Niskayuna at the corner of Rosendale Road and the Troy-Schenectady road.

Opposite, bottom: Below: After Schenectady was settled, Elias Van Guysling was the first to build a home outside the safety of the village in 1670.

living in the area called Connistigione or Nistigowone, meaning "extensive corn flats."

There were Dutch settlers farming the land as early as the 1640s, although the first documented home is that of Harmon Vedder in 1664.

The town was enlarged in 1853 when Niskayuna annexed the area around Grand Boulevard and Upper Union Street from the City of Schenectady.

SCHENECTADY COUNTY AND CITY

Albany County encompassed much of upstate New York during the Colonial era, but in March of 1772 it was subdivided, creating the now extinct counties of Tryon (west of Schenectady) and Charlotte (east and north).

Its size reduction continued in 1786 and in 1791, when Rensselaer and Saratoga Counties were formed, and again in 1809 when Schenectady

Above: A steam locomotive roars through Athens Junction early in the twentieth century.

Below: A county planning board map from 1984 shows how Schenectady County is divided into its five towns, and the City.

Bottom right: A map of Schenectady from 1798 when it was incorporated as a city.

County was created. It is bounded on the east and north by Saratoga County, while to the south and west are Albany and Schoharie Counties, and to the northwest Montgomery County.

Schenectady County is 25 miles long and 20 miles wide at its greatest dimensions, measuring 206 square miles in area, which makes it the second smallest county in the state outside of New York City. County residents, according to the 2000 U.S. Census, number 146,555, making it twenty-second in population among the 62 counties making up the state.

Schenectady itself was granted certain municipal rights back in 1684 and was chartered

as a borough in 1765. It became a district in March of 1772, and was incorporated as a township in the county of Albany in 1788. Finally, in March of 1798, Schenectady became a city.

Schenectady was divided into four wards, the first two comprising what is generally now the city limits, while the third and fourth wards became Rotterdam and Glenville, respectively, in 1820.

Today, Schenectady covers 11.0 square miles and has 61,821 people according to the 2000 U.S. census, making it the ninth largest city in the state.

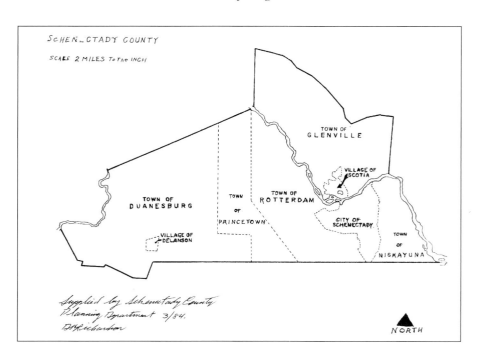

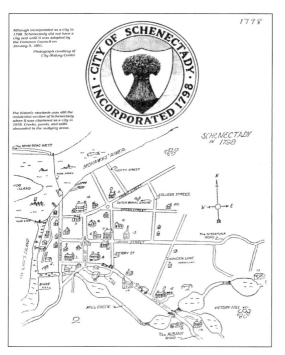

CHAPTER IV

PREACHING AND TEACHING

CHURCHES

This painting of the 1813 building by Samuel Sexton is based on Giles Yates' drawing.

By 1794, more than 10 years after the American colonies had earned their freedom from Great Britain and almost 20 years after the signing of the Declaration of Independence, the sermons at the First Reformed Church in Schenectady were still delivered in Dutch. English had been the official language in New York for more than one hundred years, but the Dutch influence was still strong and old habits died hard.

However, when a small group of church members, including future mayor and governor Joseph Yates, suggested it was time for the pastor to begin using English on Sunday mornings, the consistory and the Reverend Dirck Romeyn, the senior minister since 1784, didn't balk at the idea. The transition wasn't an entirely smooth one, though, and after initially deciding to offer English sermons every Sunday, the consistory determined that every other Sunday made more sense. In 1798, the year Schenectady became incorporated as a city with Yates appointed as its first mayor, English was clearly becoming the more common language among the townsfolk while Dutch was on the wane. With both the nearby St. George's Episcopal and First Presbyterian Church offering sermons in English, the First Reformed was in danger of losing its younger members and seeing its numbers dwindle.

Fortunately, Reverend Romeyn was a man of vision, in educational as well as spiritual matters. The individual as responsible as anyone for the formation of Union College in 1795, Romeyn's ministry helped the First Reformed maintain its standing as a vital part of the Schenectady community. When Romeyn died in his sixtieth year, on April 16, 1804, English had become the official language of the church. It was very likely Romeyn himself who delivered the final sermon in Dutch earlier that year.

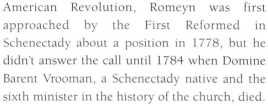

❖

Above: The First Reformed Church at the corner of Church and Union Streets as it looked in the 1880s.

Below: A 1734 image shows the First Reformed's third edifice, which stood next to the present church.

Born in Hackensack, New Jersey, in January of 1744, and heavily influenced by his older brother Thomas, also a Reformed minister, Romeyn attended Princeton University (then the College of New Jersey) and graduated in 1765. He began his ministerial career by returning home to serve churches in Hackensack and Schraalenbergh. A strong supporter of the American Revolution, Romeyn was first approached by the First Reformed in Schenectady about a position in 1778, but he didn't answer the call until 1784 when Domine Barent Vrooman, a Schenectady native and the sixth minister in the history of the church, died.

Romeyn immediately went to work in Schenectady trying to improve the educational prospects of its young citizens, his goal of an academy and a seminary eventually leading to the formation of Union College eleven years after his arrival. Between his ministry at First Reformed and his endeavors in education, Romeyn's contributions to his adopted hometown at the turn of the eighteenth century make him one of the most important citizens in Schenectady's long history.

The man seemed universally respected by everyone he came in contact with, as a letter from DeWitt Clinton, then governor of New York, to Romeyn's son John Brodhead Romeyn, clearly revealed: "I had frequent occasion, from my official situation, to see your father, and what I have said of him was an expression of the head as well as the heart, in favor of eminent merit. There was something in his manner, peculiarly dignified and benevolent, calculated to create veneration as well as affection, and it made an impression on my mind that will never be erased."

The First Reformed in Schenectady is one of the oldest congregations in the U.S., having been formed some time after Schenectady's founding and before Alexander Lindsay Glen built the first church building in 1682. The building now located on the corner of Union and North Church Street is the sixth in the church's history. A 1948 fire didn't completely destroy the exterior and the structure looks a lot like the one designed by Edward Tuckerman Potter in 1863 on the same site. Along with Romeyn, the First Reformed has had a number of distinguished pastors, including noted historian William E. Griffis (1877-86), Schenectady's socialist mayor George Lunn (1904-1909), and Clark V. Poling (1938-43), one of the "Four Chaplins" who went down with his ship in the North Atlantic during World War II.

The oldest church building in Schenectady is St. George's Episcopal, which was built from 1759-62 with money donated by William Johnson. The Reverend John Miller was an Episcopal minister who began giving sermons in the village as far back as 1695, while the current congregation dates back to 1735.

St. George's was something of a loyalist stronghold during the American Revolution, many of its English congregants feeling an emotional attachment to the mother country. According to Willis Hanson's *A History of Schenectady During the Revolution*, "in the English Church (St. George's), while many of the indignities suffered by her sister churches had been escaped, desolation now prevailed. The building, dilapidated, with windows broken out, had even become the resort of swine that roamed at will through the streets of the town. Of those congregants who had attended service before the war but a few remained, upon whom, as courage revived, devolved the burden of restoring the church building and renewing parochial activities."

St. George's was built with the help of a small group of Scotsmen who brought to Schenectady its third denomination, the Presbyterians. There was an agreement between the two congregations that the Presbyterians

would also use St. George's, "the former (the Episcopalians) to Goe in at the west door and the latter (the Presbyterians) at the south door." This arrangement was short-lived. At some point in the first decade after the St. George's building was finished, friction developed between the two groups and by 1770, the Presbyterians were gathering again in a private residence and had begun building their own house of worship near the rear of St. George's property. When that small chapel was torn down in 1809, the Presbyterians began meeting at the nearby Union College Chapel while their

St. George's Episcopal Church, shown here early in the 20th century, is the oldest church building in Schenectady, dating back to 1759.

new building, the current church on Union Street, was built on the same site.

The Methodists were the fourth denomination to make an appearance in Schenectady, organizing in 1807 and building their current church on the corner of State Street and Lafayette Street in 1874. The Baptists were well organized by the 1820s, and in 1830, the first Catholic congregation, St. John the Baptist, was meeting and would put up its current building on Franklin Street in 1839. A Jewish community also sprang up in the first half of the 19th century with the Congregation Gates of Heaven, organizing in 1854.

UNION COLLEGE

When Romeyn, Yates, and other prominent Schenectadians finally secured a charter to form Union College in 1795, Eliphalet Nott was spending his final year at Brown University, soon to graduate with the degree of master of arts. A year later he was a pastor at a small Presbyterian church in Cherry Valley, and in 1798 he moved to Albany to become a pastor at

First Presbyterian Church. It was from that pulpit that Nott gave an impassioned criticism of dueling following the death of friend and Founding Father Alexander Hamilton in his confrontation with Aaron Burr. Nott's address was reported in newspapers across the country, creating such a public fervor against dueling that the practice was eventually outlawed. Although a gifted public orator, Nott's first love was teaching, not preaching, and in 1804 he was chosen to be president of Union College, succeeding John Blair Smith (1795-1799), Jonathan Edwards (1799-1801), and Jonathan Maxcy (1802-1804).

Over the next six decades, Nott became synonymous with Union College, the name indicating its nondenominational status as the city's three churches, the First Reformed, St. George's, and the First Presbyterian, were all an integral part of its formation. Nott remained president even after suffering a paralytic stroke in 1859, and died on January 29, 1866, at the age of ninety-two.

Nott created a lottery to help Union through some hard financial times, a maneuver Union

professor and historian Jonathan Pearson called a "devil's contract." Some historians have suggested that Nott's reign was too long, his clinging to power with the help of his wife Urania causing the school to lose its prestigious academic standing over the second half of the nineteenth century.

Pearson, who was appointed treasurer of the school under Nott, had nearly as long a career at the school as the president. A Union graduate in 1835, Pearson immediately became a tutor at the school and by 1839 was a professor of natural history. Along with his duties as treasurer (from 1854-1883), Pearson continued teaching until his death at the age of 74 in 1887.

The 19th oldest college in the nation, Union celebrated its 200th anniversary in 1995 and continues to be a vital part of the Schenectady community. Its most noted alumnus is our nation's twentieth president, Chester A. Arthur.

Celebrating its fortieth anniversary in 2009 is Schenectady County Community College, a two-year school and part of the State University of New York system. Established in 1967 by the Schenectady County Board of Representatives,

Opposite, top, left: The First Presbyterian Church of Schenectady, built around 1810, still looks a lot like it does in this photograph from the 1960s.

Opposite, top right: The First United Methodist Church was built at the corner of State and Lafayette Street in 1874.

Opposite, bottom: Union College students pose for the camera outside the Nott Memorial on campus during the 1880s.

Below: An 1872 photograph shows a section of Schenectady as well as the Union College campus in the distance, before the Nott Memorial was completed.

Clockwise from top right:

This photograph from 1925 shows construction being done on the Hotel Van Curler.

The Hotel Van Curler, as it looked in 1930, became Schenectady County Community College in 1969.

Jonathan Pearson was a long-time professor and treasurer for Union College, as well as one of Schenectady's top historians of the nineteenth century.

Eliphalet Nott ruled as president of Union College for more than sixty years.

the college began holding classes in September of 1969 in the building previously known as the Hotel Van Curler. The permanent campus, located near the Mohawk River, underwent major additions in 1978 and 1987.

Schenectady's public schools began with Romeyn's brainchild in 1785, and by 1807 Schenectady also had an academy for females. New York State, which set the pace for public education throughout the country, was offering free schooling for poor children by 1809, and by 1818 Schenectady had adopted a system designed by English schoolmaster Joseph Lancaster.

In 1854 the city reorganized the system after a model begun in nearby Troy, and in 1857 had built its first high school. As Schenectady continued to grow, schools were added, and just after the turn of the century, eight new buildings, including Nott Terrace High School, were built. Under the leadership of Charles Steinmetz, the GE scientific genius who became school board president, and George Lunn, elected Schenectady's only Socialist mayor in 1912, the city's schools continued to experience growth. In 1931 Mont Pleasant High School was built, Linton High replaced Nott Terrace in 1957, and in 1992 the two schools merged on Linton's campus to form Schenectady High School.

CHAPTER V

THE NINETEENTH CENTURY

CLINTON AND YATES

Imagine how Joseph Yates must have felt. Here it was, September of 1831, and while his political career was over, he was still held in high esteem by many of his fellow Schenectadians and New Yorkers. As a former governor of the state and mayor of Schenectady, Yates was invited to take a ride on a new mode of transportation, a rail car propelled by steam engine. This novel contrivance, a railroad, was taking Yates and a handful of other dignitaries on a fifteen-mile journey from Albany to Schenectady.

While it must have been an exciting occasion for everyone involved, it had to be bittersweet for Yates. The steam engine propelling these three stagecoaches on rails was named for his political rival, DeWitt Clinton.

This painting of Joseph Yates, done by John Vanderlyn around 1815, belongs to New York's City Hall.

Undoubtedly the most influential New Yorker in the first three decades of the nineteenth century, Clinton had originally been an ally of Yates as the Schenectadian's career journey took him from his uncle's law office in Albany to a spot on the New York State supreme court.

As things turned out, Yates might have been happier remaining in the judicial branch of government, because he was not the politician Clinton was. While Clinton maneuvered and manipulated his way to the governorship of New York and nearly became president of the United States, losing narrowly to James Madison in 1812, Yates plodded through politics, winning the state office in 1822, but then quickly falling out of favor with the voters. Clinton, meanwhile, resurrected his career, sandwiching his first two terms and his third and fourth terms as governor around Yates' one term. While Clinton seemed to know the pulse of the populace and reacted to it swiftly, Yates,

though well-meaning and genuine, wasn't so quick to adapt and suddenly found himself on the wrong side of an issue—popular elections —which effectively ended his political career.

But in 1831 Yates had at last conquered Clinton in one aspect; he would live longer. Clinton had died on February 11, 1828, at the age of 58, while Yates lived until 1837, passing away at the age of 69. Clinton had taken much of the credit, and deservedly so, for the success of the Erie Canal a few years earlier, and now on this occasion, when Schenectady was again playing such a vital role in New York's history, Clinton would again, from the grave, steal the spotlight from Joseph Yates. The *DeWitt Clinton*, built at a West Point foundry, wasn't the first steam engine to transport passengers by rail, but it was the first to make it perfectly clear that railroads would be the biggest innovation in transportation in the nineteenth century.

THE CANAL

The first three decades of the nineteenth century were a time of tremendous change in Schenectady. Two years before the turn of the century, 1798, the town had been incorporated as a city and Joseph Yates had been selected as mayor by governor John Jay. Schenectady had been thriving since the American Revolution, establishing itself in the boat-building industry due to its location on the Mohawk. The river, much wider but also shallower than it is today, was not navigable from Albany to Schenectady, and the way west also offered plenty of challenges. Boat builders like Jacob Glen, Stephen Bayard, and Jonathan Walton and their factories along the Binnekill, a branch of the Mohawk, were kept busy producing all kinds of river craft, including one particularly effective vessel called the *Schenectady Durham*. It was bateau-like in many ways, between 50 and 60 feet long and eight to 10 feet wide, with a partial deck fore and aft. Flat on the bottom with a slight curve from bow to stern, its empty weight was only about 3,000 pounds, but it could carry up to 20 tons of cargo.

Though it sported a mast for square-rigged sails, a Durham was usually propelled upstream by men wielding eighteen-foot iron-tipped poles. It became very popular during the War of

This painting of New York governor DeWitt Clinton is by Schenectady's Samuel Sexton. It is part of the Union College collection.

1812 as the American army mounted numerous western excursions from the shores of the Mohawk at Schenectady.

In 1815 a Schenectadian by the name of Eri Lusher had a daily line of packet boats carrying passengers from Schenectady out to Utica. They were designed in much the same manner as the Durham boat, but included a cabin "curtained and cushioned," according to nineteenth-century Schenectady historian Austin Yates. Capable of carrying between 20 and 30 passengers, Lusher's boats made the trip to Utica in about two days, but could return to Schenectady, with favorable wind and current, in only thirteen hours.

While this mode of transportation seemed fine to some and was undoubtedly easier than taking a land route west, a few notable businessmen were always looking for something better, a more efficient and faster way to get their goods to their customers. The first serious attempt to quicken the transporting of goods on the Mohawk came in 1792 when the Western Inland Lock and Navigation Company was formed. Philip Schuyler and two associates,

Goldsbrow Banger and Elkanah Watson, went on a mission to scout the Mohawk and determine what exactly had to be done to make the river more navigable.

Their report to the company's board of directors gives us a good look into what the river actually looked like more than two hundred years ago.

"From the preceding description of the river, the board will readily perceive that from Schenectady to the mouth of the Schoharie Creek, the obstructions are many, from the number of rapids, the little water on those rapids and above them. Several of the rapids might be deepened by erecting small stone dams, nearly across the river, leaving a passage for boats; but this, whilst it would give a sufficiency of water, would also increase its velocity as to render an ascent with a half-loaded boat, of a size to carry 30 or 40 bushels of wheat, extremely difficult, without the aid of machinery to draw up the boat, and such machinery it would be difficult to permanently erect on account of the vast quantity of ice

This nineteenth-century illustration shows what boating on the Mohawk River looked like from 1797-1825.

which suddenly descends whenever the Schoharie Creek breaks up in the spring of the year, and which would destroy such machinery."

Work on the Mohawk to make it more navigable began in 1793, but the project plodded along for years and never really got going, finishing as a financial failure for all those who put money into it. It did, however, plant a seed that would develop into the Erie Canal less than three decades later.

The Mohawk Turnpike, meanwhile, incorporated as a toll road in 1800, helped spawn the building of numerous inns and taverns along the river, sometimes averaging at least one every mile from Schenectady to Utica. Those establishments, at least the ones fortunate enough to be built along the path of the Erie Canal, flourished throughout the first half of the nineteenth century.

The Erie Canal, "Clinton's Ditch," was not without its naysayers. Also called "Clinton's Folly" during its construction, the negativity surrounding the project was the primary reason Clinton didn't return to the governor's seat in

1822 and didn't even bother to run, leaving Yates to win the office by a landslide over Solomon Southwick. The tally was 128,493 votes for Yates and just 2,910 for Southwick— 98 percent to 2 percent in Yates' favor—and it appeared that the sentiment of President James Madison a few years earlier that the canal, was "a century too soon," was right. Even his predecessor in office, Thomas Jefferson, refused to give the project any federal funds, saying "it is a splendid project, and may be executed a century hence." Jefferson and Madison were both wrong. As sections of the canal opened it soon became apparent that "Clinton's Ditch" was going to be a big success.

By October 26, 1825, the canal's official ceremonial opening, Clinton was back in the governor's office. He was on hand in Buffalo to board the *Seneca Chief*, a small packboat, as it left the lock and headed to Albany. The departure was accompanied by cannon fire, which was repeated all along the canal, each shot within hearing range of the prior one, and it continued past Albany down the Hudson to

Albany area artist Len Tantillo painted this scene of the Schenectady Harbor.

Sandy Hook just outside of New York. The volley of cannon, serving as a signal to those in Sandy Hook that Clinton and the *Seneca Chief* were on their way, took an hour and 20 minutes.

Clinton and his party were greeted with great pomp and ceremony along the way, although not every community felt so celebratory. In Rome, drummers beat on muffled drums as the boat passed and officials poured a keg of black water into the canal.

In Schenectady, though officials did greet the group and dinner was provided for them at Givens' Hotel, the mood was also subdued. There's no record of Schenectady participating in the cannon-firing that skipped along the canal path, but a group of Union College cadets reportedly fired a couple of volleys in honor of the occasion.

Why did Schenectady lack enthusiasm for the canal, deemed by some at the time to be the "eighth wonder of the world?" Schenectady had prospered since the American Revolution, not only as a boat manufactury but also as one of the new nation's leading producers of brooms. Farmers throughout the area, particularly in Scotia, were growing special broom corn that was tall and had tough, fibrous tassels. The business of broom-making flourished throughout the 19th century and lasted well into the 20th century, the Whitmyer Broom Factory on Front Street in Schenectady remaining in operation up until the 1970s.

It wasn't brooms or its boat-building prowess, however, that made Schenectady the "gateway to the west." It was its location on the Mohawk River, a resource the country used to its

Above: Popular Albany area artist Len Tantillo painted this scene of the early days of the Erie Canal.

Below: This nineteenth-century illustration shows the DeWitt Clinton making its first run from Albany to Schenectady in 1831.

This Samuel Sexton painting from the mid-nineteenth century shows Dock Street in Schenectady right along the Erie Canal.

advantage during the War of 1812, that made the Dutch town so important. With the coming of the canal, however, instead of being the primary embarkation point westward, Schenectady would become just another town.

The Great Fire of 1819 destroyed the boat-building business along the Binnekill, a branch of the Mohawk that bordered the city, and that section of Schenectady never recovered its commercial prestige. When Clinton and his party made their way to Schenectady in 1825, city officials, still reeling from the Great Fire, could see the handwriting on the wall. Schenectady's days as a key starting point to the way west were numbered.

THE RAILROAD

As successful as the canal was, it still took a long time for boats to make their way through the numerous locks between Waterford and Schenectady.

For George W. Featherstonhaugh, an Englishman who had come to the country in

1806 after graduating from Oxford, time was money and they were both being wasted. As early as December of 1825, just two months after Clinton's triumphant opening of the canal, Featherstonhaugh published a notice in the *Schenectady Cabinet*, one of the city's first newspapers, of his intentions of incorporating a railroad. Featherstonhaugh had seen steam locomotives in England and saw no reason why a rail line "betwixt the Mohawk and Hudson Rivers," an overland track that would bypass the slower canal route between Albany to Schenectady, would not work.

Featherstonhaugh was the lone voice for railroads until he enlisted the support of one of Albany's most prominent citizens, Stephen Van Rensselaer. Then, on April 17, 1826, the New York assembly agreed and the Mohawk-Hudson Railroad Company was born.

Work on the line didn't begin until July 29, 1830, but by the following summer 12 miles of double track had been laid from the outskirts of Albany to the bluffs just southwest of Schenectady. The first trial run, on Aug 1, 1831,

left Albany and reached Schenectady an hour and 45 minutes later, coming to a stop at a point called Engine Hill near the top of Crane Street. Nearly two months later, Yates and John Isaac DeGraff, a U.S. congressman from Schenectady, were among the dignitaries welcomed aboard by conductor Billy Marshall on September 24, 1831, for the *DeWitt Clinton's* first grand excursion.

In 1832 the Schenectady to Saratoga Railroad was completed, followed by a line from Schenectady to Utica in 1836 and another from Schenectady to Troy in 1843. With the success of the Mohawk and Hudson Railroad, similar lines were popping up all over the eastern half of the U.S., but Schenectady, with four railroads converging within its limits, was a giant of rail transportation. Within two decades it would also become one of the nation's top manufacturers of steam locomotives, a business that would help keep the city thriving for close to a hundred more years. Like the canal, which it was initially only meant to supplement, not replace, the railroad didn't come without its

share of criticism. Martin Van Buren, who in 1829 was governor of New York, wrote to then-President John Quincy Adams opining that to sink any federal money into the venture would be a big mistake.

"The canal system of this country is being threatened by a new form of transportation known as railroads...as you may well know, Mr. President, railroad carriages are pulled at enormous speeds of 15 miles per hour by engines which, in addition to endangering the life and limb of passengers, roar and snort their way through the countryside, setting fire to crops, scaring the livestock and frightening woman and children. The Almighty certainly never intended that people should travel at such breakneck speed." Van Buren, who had earlier also been an opponent of the Erie Canal, was wrong again. The canal continued to prosper, the railroad business flourished, and Schenectady reaped the dividends. While the rise of the railroad around the country almost immediately began to have negative effects on canal business, in New York the Erie Canal

Rufus Grider, a nineteenth-century artist and Canajoharie school teacher, visited Schenectady in 1890, researched its history, and sketched this scene of the Binnekill, a branch of the Mohawk River at Schenectady as it would have looked in 1790.

Right: This painting by nineteenth-century artist Samuel Sexton shows lower State Street and the law office of John Isaac DeGraff.

Below: George Featherstonhaugh, one of Duanesburg's top citizens, was the man behind the birth of the railroad.

Bottom: Cadwallader Clute was owner of the Clute Brothers factory in Schenectady that helped build the Union Civil Warship the Monitor.

continued to thrive, reaching its peak in tonnage in 1872 and continuing to turn a profit until 1883.

Eventually, Van Buren would be right about the threat the railroad posed, but the canal survived into the second decade of the twentieth century, and its successor, the New York State Barge Canal, still transports some goods up and down the river—although much of the traffic these days is recreational. The railroad, meanwhile, proved that Featherstonhaugh's vision would have the most far-reaching impact, changing the way Americans thought about travel and making rail traffic the premier mode of transportation through the first half of the twentieth century.

Featherstonhaugh, however, never really got to bask in the success of the railroad. The man who had saved the daughter of James Duane from two out-of-control horses on a street in Philadelphia in 1806, married her two years later at St. George's Episcopal Church in Schenectady, and had then taken up residence in Duanesburg, was dealt some cruel blows in 1826. Just a short time after his dream of rail traffic was given the stamp of approval by the state legislature, Featherstonhaugh lost both his daughters and his wife to illness. He returned to England following their deaths, but came back to the U.S. in 1831 and got married again in

Schenectady County. He and his new wife named one of their daughters Albany.

Earlier, in 1829, Featherstonhaugh had resigned from the board of directors of the Mohawk and Hudson Railroad and had little to do with the project after that. He also sold his considerable share in the venture, and was not among the invited guests on the *DeWitt Clinton's* initial trip that summer of 1831.

He was not, however, done with his contribution to the America push westward. In 1834 he was named the first official U.S. Government Geologist and spent much of that decade surveying the Louisiana Purchase.

Whether Featherstonhaugh became disillusioned with the railroad or just distracted by personal tragedies, men like Joseph Yates and John Isaac DeGraff more than filled the void left by his absence, ensuring the success of the Mohawk and Hudson Railroad. DeGraff was a lawyer and prominent businessman who had served his country during the War of 1812 and whose fortune helped build the U.S. Navy during that same critical period. He was elected to the U.S. Congress in 1829 as a Jacksonian Democrat and was asked by President Van Buren to become his secretary of the treasury, an offer he declined. He went back to Congress in 1837 for another two-year term, but in the meantime, in 1832, DeGraff became the first

Left: This old covered bridge over the Mohawk River connecting Schenectady to Scotia was built in 1809, the year of the founding of Schenectady County, and demolished in 1874. The painting is by William Henry Yates (1845-1934).

Below: William Seward, born in Orange County, N.Y., in 1801, graduated from Union College in 1820 and became New York's governor, senator and the U.S. Secretary of State under Abraham Lincoln.

Bottom: Robert Toombs, a native of Wilkes County, Georgia, and an 1828 graduate of Union College, was the Confederate Secretary of State when the Civil War opened in 1861.

mayor of Schenectady to be elected by the people. He was voted into the office on three more occasions, the last in 1845. Three years later, on July 26, 1848, DeGraff died at the age of sixty-four.

Yates, meanwhile, was even considered a candidate for vice-president during his honeymoon period in the governor's office. It didn't happen, but while Yates' ability as a politician was often questioned, no one doubted his motives.

"Judge Yates was an honest man, possessed of a good understanding, who always designed to do what he thought was right," wrote Van Buren in his autobiography. "He warded off too strict a scrutiny into his mental capacities by a dignified and prudent reserve—a policy that long practice had made second nature."

THE CIVIL WAR

Newland Holmes, Jr., Union College class of '61, was probably ringleader of the group responsible for shenanigans that made their appearance in Schenectady that spring.

One of the few remaining Southern students on campus during spring break in April of 1861, Holmes never made it back to Union for the graduation ceremonies in June. Instead, when the news reached Schenectady that Fort Sumter had been fired upon by the Confederacy on April 12, Holmes and a group of around 10 students, all Southerners, immediately left for home, taking the first train out of the city after midnight.

They didn't leave quietly. While there is no documentation from contemporary sources, the group reputedly showed where their loyalties lay before heading to the train station by writing the South Carolina motto "Animus Opibusque Parati," ("Prepared in Mind and Resources"), on a number of classroom blackboards. They also raised a Confederate flag on the city flagpole at Liberty and Ferry Streets.

Holmes, a New Orleans native, wound up serving as a colonel in the Confederate Army and was listed as missing at the end of the Civil War. But he wasn't the only Union College casualty of the war. Not by a long shot.

In the fall of 1860, Schenectady had long been a Democratic town and that wasn't about to change. While Union College president Eliphalet Nott voted for the Republican candidate, Abraham Lincoln, he was in the minority.

Although Schenectady was cool toward the new president and certainly didn't embrace the abolition of slavery, most of the city's population of 9,500 felt strongly about the Union. Before the month of April was over, Schenectady had formed one company of men commanded by William Seward Gridley, and in May Captain Stephen Truax had put together another company. Both groups served with the 18th Regiment of New York Volunteers, and in July, when Union and Confederate troops met at Bull Run in the first major confrontation of the Civil War, both Schenectady companies were there. A third and fourth company of men would be recruited from Schenectady County before the summer was done, and by July of 1863 the county had 450 men serving in the 134th Infantry, part of the Potomac Army that was heavily engaged at Gettysburg.

Meanwhile, at Union College that first spring, students returning from their break in April rallied to the cause, professor Elias Peissner taking the initiative to form a group of eighty-two young men and drill them and see that they received instructions on military strategy. About fifty of the Union College Zouaves, as they were called, earned commissions in the Union army, while Peissner, married with two young children, ended up serving as Colonel in the 119th New York Regiment, which headed to war in July of 1862.

Union College's involvement in the Civil War didn't end with the contribution made by its students-turned-soldiers. Remarkably, both men serving as Secretary of State when the war began, William Seward for the Union and Robert Toombs for the Confederacy, were Union College alumni.

Seward, born in Orange County, New York, in 1801, graduated from Union in 1820 and passed the state's bar exam in 1821. He moved to Auburn in central New York in 1823, quickly rose through the ranks of state politics, and by 1838 was elected governor of the state as a member of the Whig party. He became a U.S. senator from New York in 1848 and played a prominent role in the formation of the Republican Party. For many, Seward seemed the likely Republican candidate for president in 1860, but as an ardent abolitionist he couldn't unite the party, allowing Lincoln to secure the nomination.

While Seward remained in his post throughout the war and became a close confidant and supporter of Lincoln, Toombs' time in the Confederate cabinet was short-lived. Like Seward, Toombs had higher ambitions than his U.S. Senate seat from Georgia, and when he resigned from that post on February 4, 1861, his ambition was to become chief executive of the Confederate States of America. Unlike Seward, however, when Jefferson Davis was selected the Confederate president, Toombs didn't play the part of second fiddle very well. He became an outspoken critic of that administration, despite the fact that Davis appointed him Secretary of State. Toombs' tenure lasted just three months before he resigned to command a brigade of Georgian troops. That endeavor also came to a quick end when Toombs, denied a promotion, resigned and returned home to Washington, Georgia.

Born on July 2, 1810, in Wilkes County, Georgia, Toombs had come from a prominent slave-holding family. A gifted student, he enrolled at the University of Georgia at the age of 14, but after a discipline problem there he transferred to Union College. Toombs graduated from Union in 1828, studied law at the University of Virginia, and embarked on a career in politics when he was elected to the U.S. House of Representatives as a Whig in 1844. Toombs became close friends with fellow Georgian Alexander Stephens, future vice-president of the Confederacy, and developed into a strong advocate of states' rights. After the demise of the Whig party, Toombs joined the

Moses Viney, who died in 1909, is shown in this photograph from 1900 with the horse and carriage he used to transport prominent Schenectadians around the city.

Constitutional Union Party in the early 1850s, and when that party began to dissolve he reluctantly became a Democrat, serving as U.S. Senator from Georgia from 1853 until his resignation eight years later.

At the conclusion of the Civil War, Toombs headed to Cuba to avoid arrest by U.S. troops. He came back to the country through Canada in 1867, but because he refused to request a pardon from Congress, he never regained his U.S. citizenship. Toombs, however, did resume a lucrative law practice and once again got involved in politics, dominating Georgia's constitutional convention of 1877. Labeled an "unreconstructed" southerner, Toombs regained his reputation as a skilled and genial politician after the Civil War, and died in December of 1885.

There's no record of him ever returning to Schenectady, and sadly, a similar fate awaited Peissner. While he did return home on a short furlough early in 1863, Peissner was killed at the Battle of Chancellorsville in May of that year. Only a few months earlier Peissner had survived the carnage at Fredericksburg, where, according to members of his unit, he was the first Union soldier to cross the Rappahannock at Kelly's Ford. Peissner was initially buried on the battlefield that day but his body was exhumed and returned home to Schenectady. According to the Union College Encyclopedia, he is the only faculty member from the school to die in military service.

The war, meanwhile, began to look like an inevitable Northern victory during the late summer of 1864. Union alum Henry "Old Brains" Halleck (class of '37) served as overall commander of the Union army early during the conflict, and was then Lincoln's chief of staff, a demotion, when William Tecumseh Sherman burned Atlanta just a few weeks before the 1864 presidential election.

Despite all the positive news on the war front, Schenectady County still voted against Lincoln and for General George McClellan, the former leader of the Army of the Potomac, giving him 2,169 votes to Lincoln's 2,103. The state as a whole, however, went for Lincoln— as did the nation, 2,330,552 to 1,835,985.

No conversation involving Schenectady's role in the Civil War is complete without mention of the Clute Brothers. Their foundry and machine shop, started by their father, Peter Clute, was one of Schenectady's most successful businesses throughout the middle third of the nineteenth century. The company's key contribution during the War Between the States was the manufacture of the steam engine that powered the turret of the *Monitor*, the Union ironclad that battled its Confederate counterpart, the *Merrimac*, to a draw off the Virginia coast on March 9, 1862. After the war, competition from the Schenectady Locomotive Works and George Westinghouse & Company made business a bit tougher for Cadwallader C. Clute and his brothers. The business failed in 1882, six years after the death of Cadwallader.

BLACKS IN NEW YORK

The Civil War and the Thirteenth Amendment, signed into law on December 6, 1865, by president Andrew Johnson, brought slavery to an end in the U.S., but in the state of New York, the "peculiar institution" had devolved into extinction back in 1827.

Moses Viney, born a slave in Maryland in 1817, came to Schenectady and worked for Union College President Eliphalet Nott.

Above: Broom corn grows in an open field along the old Mohawk Bridge sometime before the bridge was demolished in 1874.

Below: The Western Gateway Bridge linking Schenectady and Scotia over the Mohawk River was completed in 1925.

Freedom, however, had came at a slow and laborious pace. In 1781, New York offered to manumit all slaves who had served in the American Revolution, and in 1799 the state legislature passed 'gradual abolition,' allowing all children born to slave women after July 4 of that year to become free. Emancipation, however, wouldn't happen for black females until they were 25, and black males had to wait until they were 28. Then, in 1817, the state decided that all blacks born before July 4, 1799, would be free, but not until July 4, 1827.

The evil of slavery had already been outlawed in the Netherlands when the Dutch first came to America, but they hadn't yet eradicated it in their colonies around the world. While suggesting that blacks had it better in the North than those in the South is problematical, there are numerous examples of slaves who remained as workers for their masters who had freed them, while others were allowed the opportunity to hire themselves out on occasion and eventually buy their freedom. In his book, "*A History of Negro Slavery in New York,*" Edgar J. McManus wrote, "The pragmatic Dutch regarded slavery as an economic expedient, they never equated it with social organization or race control."

On January 10, 1909, one of Schenectady's last links to slavery, Moses Viney, died at his home at 229 Lafayette Street. Viney's story, which began in slavery in Maryland in 1817, is a remarkable one. His flight to freedom, first to Philadelphia, then to New York City and finally Schenectady, wasn't easy, but by 1842 he was in the employ of Union College president Eliphalet Nott. Viney served as Nott's coachman and personal servant, and long after Nott's death continued to work, transporting college officials and alumni around the campus and city in the horse and carriage he had purchased from Nott's wife.

ONE DOLLAR FINE FOR CROSSING THIS BRIDGE FASTER THAN ON A WALK.

CHAPTER VI

"THE CITY THAT LIGHTS AND HAULS THE WORLD"

GE AND ALCO

Thomas Edison was offering $37,500 for the tract of land just west of town, but N. I. Schermerhorn and the Stanford family were asking $45,000. Both parties refused to budge.

Fortunately, city leaders like Colonel Robert Furman realized what a great opportunity was being presented to Schenectady in June of 1886—it was rumored that Edison's new plant might employ 1,000 workers—and the money needed to seal the deal, $7,500, was collected from more than 100 prominent citizens.

Schenectady's prosperous future—it would become known as the "city that lights and hauls the world"—was secured. The General Electric Company and the American Locomotive Company, (ALCO), sometimes in cooperation and often in competition, would make Schenectady a prominent member of the world-wide technological community throughout the first half of the twentieth century. But it almost didn't happen.

While it is impossible to talk about either GE or ALCO without including the other, any conversation about their inception has to start with John Ellis. Born in Garmouth, Scotland, on December 13, 1795, Ellis arrived in America in 1831 as a master mechanic, and two decades later was the head business agent of the Schenectady Locomotive Works. Incorporated in 1851, Ellis's company ensured that railroad history in Schenectady wouldn't begin and end with the 1831 run of the *DeWitt Clinton*. The Schenectady Locomotive Engine Manufactory, a company started by the Norris brothers of Philadelphia in 1848, was on the verge of failing before Ellis moved in and

The Ellis home, shown in this 1876 photograph, was on the corner of Union Street and Nott Terrace.

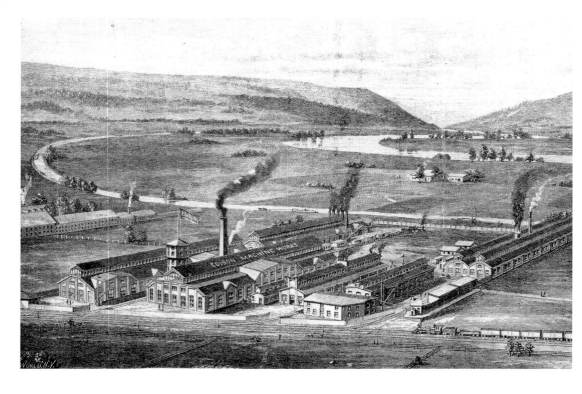

reorganized the business and changed its name to the Schenectady Locomotive Works. The new business prospered under Ellis's leadership and would remain the city's largest company throughout the second half of the nineteenth century. Ellis died in 1864 and left the business in the hands of his three capable sons.

Each of them, John C., Charles G., and William had a run at serving as president, but it was William who was in charge in 1901 when the company merged with seven other locomotive builders to form the American Locomotive Company.

Under the guidance of the Ellis brothers, ALCO developed into the largest builder of locomotives in the world in the twentieth century. Before it was ALCO, the Schenectady Locomotive Works built the *Jupiter*, one of the Central Pacific Railroad locomotives that participated in the joining of the Transcontinental Railroad at Promontory, Utah, in 1869. A key figure in the company's success was Walter McQueen, whose name became synonymous with the engines produced at Schenectady ("McQueen Engines"). However, during Charles Ellis's tenure (1878-91), McQueen's long stint as plant manager was interrupted due to a falling-out between the two. In 1885, with financial backing from Charles Stanford, McQueen decided to start his own locomotive-building plant, and two shops were built on 12 acres of land owned by Schermerhorn on the flats just west of Schenectady.

However, when Stanford suffered losses in the stock market, he was unable to continue financing the project. With things in limbo, McQueen was able to get his old job back with Charles Ellis, and a short time after he left, Stanford died, forever killing the prospect of another locomotive factory in Schenectady.

It looked as if Schenectady, in 1886 a town of fourteen thousand people, might remain a city

dominated by one big business. Fate, however, and Harry M. Livor, stepped in.

Thomas Edison's Edison Machine Works, in Menlo Park, New Jersey, was suffering from labor problems as well as growing pains, and on a scouting trip through the Mohawk Valley as Edison's representative, Livor just happened to glance out the window to the right as his train left Schenectady heading south. What he saw was Schermerhorn's "big flat," occupied only by two lonely factory buildings. He quickly reported the discovery upon his return to Menlo Park, convincing Edison himself to make a special trip to Schenectady later in 1886. The inventor and industrialist liked what he saw, but he found the $45,000 figure a little steep.

With little hope for compromise on the price, Colonel Furman and John De Remer, a prominent Schenectady lawyer, sprang into action. They immediately began

soliciting contributions from other well-to-do Schenectadians, and on June 14, 1886, with De Remer in New York negotiating with Edison and Furman in Schenectady raising the cash, the Colonel wired De Remer telling him to seal the deal. The $7,500 they needed to bring Edison to Schenectady had been raised.

De Remer himself, president of the city school board and a Union College trustee, had put up $500, as did Barney & Company and another contributor who wished to remain anonymous. Colonel Furman and nine others gave $200, two more gave $150, and an

additional 43, including Charles Ellis, gave $100. According to the June 28 edition of the *Daily Union*, between 50 and 60 contributors added $25 apiece to the kitty, and a handful more contributed $10.

Within a year, Edison Machine Works had hired eight hundred workers and established Schenectady as its headquarters. According to scientific journalist T. Comerford Martin, the Schenectady works was a "vast establishment of noble machine shops…where the prosaic and marvelous jostle each other…one of the greatest exemplifications of American inventive genius." In 1892 Edison merged his company with a competitor, the Thomson-Houston Electrical Company, to form the General Electric Company. By the turn of the century, with GE and ALCO fueling a massive immigrant migration to Schenectady, the city's population had ballooned to 31,692. Amazingly, in another ten years it would more than double, the 1910 census giving a count of 72,826.

WESTINGHOUSE

GE and ALCO weren't the only businesses making Schenectady a vital part of the world's technological community at the turn of the twentieth century.

George Westinghouse, Sr., the father of the man who would make Westinghouse one of the top names in appliances throughout the world in the twentieth century, moved to Schenectady in 1856 and brought his farm implement business with him.

A native of Pownal, Vermont, Westinghouse moved to Ohio in 1831, to Minaville (near Amsterdam) in 1833, and to Central Bridge in Schoharie County in 1835. It was there he began working seriously on a threshing machine that would revolutionize the farming industry. Westinghouse's business was doing so well two decades later that he moved to Schenectady in 1856 and secured a nice location for a new factory right alongside the Erie Canal.

There his business flourished for sixty-seven years before the company was moved to another location in Shortsville, New York, in Ontario County, in 1923, long after Westinghouse's death. He died in 1884 at the age of seventy-five and is buried in Schenectady's Vale Cemetery.

His son, George, Jr., meanwhile, was born on October 6, 1846, and moved to Schenectady with his family when he was nine. Growing up in his father's factory, George, Jr., displayed a fine aptitude for science and technology, and in 1865, after serving some time in the Union army during the Civil War, Westinghouse began taking classes at Union College. He didn't find academic life to his liking, however, and spent little more than three months at Union before quitting school and going back to his father's factory.

In 1869 the younger Westinghouse broke out on his own and moved to Pittsburgh, where his business, Westinghouse Industries, eventually grew into one of the largest in the world. He died in 1914 after having registered over four hundred patents, the most notable the air brake.

STEINMETZ
AND OTHER WIZARDS

"Teaching," said Charles Proteus Steinmetz, "is the most important profession, because upon teachers depends the future of our nation, and, in fact, all civilization." If not for that sentiment, Steinmetz would have spent all of his time in the laboratory and none in the classroom. Born in 1865 in what was then Breslau, Germany, and is now Wroclaw, Poland, Steinmetz spent 30 years (1893-1923) working for GE and 11 years (1902-1913) teaching electrical engineering at Union College. His fame in the

Left: Many General Electric employees at the turn of the twentieth century got to the plant by riding a bicycle.

Below: George Westinghouse, Sr., moved his farm implement company to Schenectady in 1856. He died in 1884 and is buried in Vale Cemetery.

Bottom: Workers get the Westinghouse Thresher ready for operation sometime soon after the Civil War.

scientific community during his lifetime was second only to that of Thomas Edison, and his contributions included the discovery of the law of hysteresis, the application of complex arithmetic to the analysis of alternating current circuits, and the theory of transient phenomena and oscillations.

A condition he inherited from his father called *kyphosis*, an abnormal curvature of the spine, made Steinmetz easily recognizable as he rode his bicycle or drove his hand-controlled electric car through the streets of Schenectady. Despite his appearance, which was also marked by the cigar constantly dangling from his mouth, sometimes lit, sometimes not, Steinmetz quickly made friends in Schenectady. He

eventually became one of its most prominent citizens, his contributions to the city including time served as president of the city council and school board as well as his work at GE and Union.

Steinmetz's popularity waned during World War I—he was a socialist and a supporter of Germany before America entered the war—but he regained a measure of stardom after the war, in part for his ability to explain the ideas of Albert Einstein to the general public. Steinmetz, who said his success was due to his love of mathematics, showed Einstein around the GE plant in Schenectady in 1921, and did the same for Edison during his return to the city in 1922. Following a long

award for his work in physics. Among the many other individuals who made a notable impact at GE were Ernst Alexanderson, a pioneer in the field of radio and television, and Katherine Burr Blodgett, who in 1939 invented non-reflecting "invisible" glass.

While Steinmetz, Langmuir (born in Brooklyn), and Giaever (Norway) all moved to Schenectady to work for GE, Blodgett was a Schenectady native. Born in 1898, she and her family moved to New York City that same year following the murder of her father, a GE employee who was killed during a robbery attempt at his home. Blodgett was the first woman to receive a Ph.D. in physics from Cambridge, and the first woman hired by GE for research work in the laboratory.

While GE continued to prosper throughout the twentieth century—it employed nearly 40,000 people in the 1940s and '50s, the company eventually moved its corporate

cross-country speaking tour, he died a year later, in October of 1923, at his home on Wendell Avenue. The "Wizard of Schenectady" was only fifty-eight.

Steinmetz wasn't the only wizard working at GE. In 1932 Irving Langmuir won the Nobel Prize for his work in surface chemistry, and in 1973 Ivar Giaever became the second GE employee to capture a Nobel when he won the

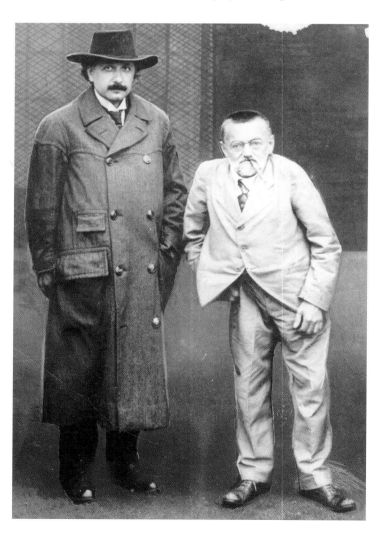

Left: Schenectady was known for much of the nineteenth century as the "broom corn capital of the world," and the biggest manufacturer was the Whitmyer Broom Company.

Below: Katherine Burr Blodgett, the first woman to earn a Ph.D in chemistry from Cambridge and the first woman hired by GE to work in the research lab, invented non-reflecting "invisible" glass.

GE scientist Irving Langmuir was presented the Nobel Prize for chemistry in 1932 by King Gustav of Sweden.

headquarters out of Schenectady and its workforce in the city has been reduced to just under 4,000.

After building seventy-five thousand diesel locomotives ALCO's long stature as a major employer in the city came to an end in 1969. In the 1930s, it was still the top producer of locomotives in the country and the Schenectady plant contributed greatly to the war effort, its 15,000 employees (an all-time high), making more than 7,000 tanks to fight Nazi Germany. In 1964 it was sold to the Worthington Corporation and five years later work at the plant came to a complete stop.

CHAPTER VII

THE TWENTIETH CENTURY

GEORGE LUNN

To some church members, Sunday mornings at the First Reformed didn't quite feel the same. The Rev. Dr. George R. Lunn was turning up the heat.

Schenectady's two big industries at the turn of the 20th century, GE and ALCO, required workers, plenty of them, and immigrants swarmed into the city to answer the call, happy to have a job and a new life in America.

But opportunity beckoned for all, and the prospects of huge profits for big business and its leaders was just as attractive. There was plenty for Dr. Lunn to see and question since moving to Schenectady and the First Reformed in 1903, and by 1909 he began asking his questions from the pulpit and pointing fingers. Lunn was bringing his social conscience to his Sunday sermons, and his oratory included more about the real world than the afterlife.

The First Reformed had always counted among its members the most prominent citizens of Schenectady, and in 1909 that was still the case, its ranks rife with corporate executives from both GE and ALCO. But big business wasn't Lunn's only target. He also harped on what he saw as abuses from the city's political community, and with members of that group also attending the First Reformed on Sundays, tensions between the minister and his flock heightened. A vote of the entire church membership supported Lunn and negated the consistory's efforts to have him replaced. However, on April 25, 1909, Lunn, not wanting to be a divisive issue within the congregation, announced his resignation, effective January 1, 1910.

Lunn didn't stop preaching, however, and instead formed his own church and lectured in front of as many as 2,000 people in a downtown theater on Sunday mornings. He also began publishing his

According to this sign, the city's population reached one hundred thousand sometime soon after 1920 although the official U.S. Census never confirmed that estimate.

Right: Soon after winning election as mayor, George Lunn was named by the Socialists as their candidate for the 30th Congress. He lost that bid, but later was elected to the U.S. House of Representatives as a Democrat.

Far right: Lucia Newell-Oliviere moved to Schenectady early in the twentieth century and joined the local Socialist Party. The mother of Jean Robert Foster, Newell-Oliviere was a social activist and a journalist, writing for George Lunn's newspaper, The Citizen.

Below: Henry S. De Forest was a mayor and U.S. congressman from Schenectady who developed much of the real estate around Central Park and the Upper Union Street area.

Opposite page, top: Dr. Elizabeth Gillette, the first woman to be elected to the New York assembly from an upstate county, practiced medicine in Schenectady for 37 years.

Opposite page, bottom: Jean Robert Foster was a poet, playwright, author, model and social worker, who in 1969 was named a Patroon by the city.

own newspaper, *The Citizen*, its first edition appearing on the streets on May 20, 1910.

Initially, he thought of himself as only a reformer without a political affiliation, but he was soon recruited by New York's Socialist Party to run for mayor. He accepted.

On November 7, 1911, the citizens of Schenectady, as well as a number of other communities around the country, were more than happy to give socialism a chance. An unhappy citizenry combined with a charismatic leader exposing the evils of municipal graft and corruption were bound to produce change, and in Schenectady a perfect storm of those elements existed.

On the national scene, Socialist leader Eugene Debs garnered nearly one million votes in the presidential election—his best showing ever in four runs at the office—and inspired Socialist Party success in state and local elections all over the U.S. In Schenectady, Debs' surrogate was Lunn, who was swept into office with eight other Socialists running for the 11 aldermanic positions in the city. The Socialists enjoyed success beyond the city limits as several Socialists were also elected to county-wide positions. But only two years later, in November of 1913, Republicans and Democrats put together a fusion ticket and defeated Lunn, J. Teller Schoolcraft taking over as mayor for a two-year term. Lunn regrouped and won again in 1916 to regain the mayoral office.

Having become disenchanted with the state Socialist Party, Lunn ran for the U.S. House of Representatives in 1917 as a Democrat and won, serving two years before returning to Schenectady and winning the mayoral election twice more. As he was beginning what was his fourth term as the city's chief executive, Lunn left the office after being elected lieutenant governor on the Democratic ticket that put Al Smith in the governor's mansion. Born in Taylor County, Iowa in 1873, Lunn retired as the state's public service commissioner in 1942 and moved to California where he died in 1948.

WOMEN OF CHANGE

Steinmetz and Lunn, responsible for creating new schools and much of the city's park systems in the first two decades of the 20th century, weren't the only people carrying the Socialist banner in Schenectady. Lucia Newell Oliviere, born Lucinda Newell in North River just before the Civil War, moved to Schenectady just before the turn of the century and was immediately attracted to the Socialists due to its policy toward women—they were treated as equals.

Oliviere, who had married a carpenter and lumberjack named Frank Oliver, stopped using Lucinda (or Lizzie, as she was often called), and also slightly changed her last name when she

moved to Schenectady. She gave lectures at Socialist meetings held in her home, often inviting others to speak on civil rights and the women's suffrage movement. She twice ran unsuccessfully on the Socialist ticket for state senator, but her agitating for underpaid women janitors at GE did help that group receive a raise in pay.

Oliviere was also a journalist, working diligently for Lunn's *The Citizen* up until her death in 1927. She wrote both editorials and breaking news stories for the newspaper, and also found the time to produce poetry and an unpublished novel.

Her egalitarian leanings had a strong effect on her daughter, Jeanne Robert Foster, who gained a measure of international fame as a poet, playwright, author, model, and social worker. Foster, a native of Johnsburg in the southern Adirondacks, was a close friend of John Butler Yeats, an artist and father of poet William Butler Yeats. She spent much of the first three decades of the 20th century traveling back and forth

across the Atlantic Ocean while working as editor for the *Review of Reviews* and American editor of the *Transatlantic Review*. In 1938, she returned to Schenectady and worked as a tenant relations counselor for the state and federal housing authorities, retiring in 1955. Foster was named a Patroon of the city by Schenectady mayor Malcolm Ellis in 1961, and in 1969, just a year before her death, she received an honorary doctor of laws degree from Union College.

Foster and her mother weren't the only women who made a difference in Schenectady in the 20th century. In 1893, Janet Murray became Schenectady's first woman doctor, running a practice out of her Mynderse Street home for four decades. Born in Peebles, Scotland, in 1856, Murray spent the last three years of her life at the Heritage Home for Women on Union Street, where she died in February of 1940.

Dr. Elizabeth Gillette, meanwhile, born in Granby, Connecticut, in 1876, got her medical

degree in New York City and came to Schenectady in 1900. While she practiced medicine in the city for 37 years, in 1919 she became the first woman elected to the state assembly from an upstate county. Gillette, also one of the first females to drive an automobile in Schenectady, lived at 254 Union Street, and died there in 1965.

TV AND RADIO

On Christmas Eve, 1906, Reginald Fessenden, a Canadian-born professor and researcher, broadcast from his station in Brant Rock, Massachusetts, the first radio transmission with music and talk. Fessenden, who played the

violin and read biblical scripture for the broadcast, used a 75 kHz alternator that was built by GE scientist Ernst Alexanderson.

Ernst Frederick Werner Alexanderson received 345 U.S. patents, the last one coming in 1968 when he was 89. Born in Sweden in 1878, Alexanderson was educated at the Royal Institute of Technology in Stockholm and the Technical University in Berlin before emigrating to the U.S. in 1902. Soon after, he began working for General Electric and played key roles in the development of both radio and television.

The Alexanderson alternator greatly enhanced the radio, and by 1922 GE had produced the

first commercial radio broadcast ever. On February 10 of that year, Kolin Hager stepped up to the mike and told his listening audience, "This is station WGY; W, the first letter in wireless, G, the first letter in General Electric, and Y, the last letter in Schenectady." Later that year WGY broadcast a college football game for the first time when Yale played Harvard at the Yale Bowl, and in 1923 WGY provided coverage of a World Series game between the New York Yankees and New York Giants from the Polo Grounds.

One medium wasn't enough for Alexanderson. While many scientists around the world were working on the transmission of visual images,

Opposite, top: This photograph of the Erie Canal and General Electric was taken in 1914 from the Washington Avenue bridge over the canal.

Opposite, left: Erie Canal looking toward General Electric.

Opposite, bottom: This photograph of downtown Schenectady was taken in 1923 from Veterans Park looking west down State Street.

Above: This 1913 photograph shows a bicyclist making his way over the Scotia Bridge into Schenectady.

Left: The New York Central Railroad began building overhead crossings in downtown Schenectady soon after the turn of the 20th Century as this 1906 photo indicates.

radio up until his retirement. He died on May 14, 1975, at the age of ninety-seven.

WRGB was originally Channel 4 on the dial, and during its infancy was known as W2XB. On February 26, 1942, its call letters were changed to WRGB in honor of GE vice-president Walter Ransom Gail Baker, an electrical engineer. A native of Lockport, New York, Baker graduated from Union College in 1916 and got a masters degree in electrical engineering from Union in 1919. A few years earlier, during World War I, he had taken a job with GE and immersed himself in the field of radio communications as they apply to military operations.

the first television broadcast in the U.S. was from Alexanderson's home at 1132 Adams Road in the GE Realty Plot. Alexanderson's work two years later in 1928 provided a picture of Alfred E. Smith's acceptance speech at the Democratic National Convention, and on November 6, 1939, WRGB began running commercial programming. Alexanderson kept right on working on improvements for both TV and

Baker was far from through with his many contributions to the industry when GE honored him by changing the call letters of its flagship station in 1942. He served as president of the National Television System Committee, and in 1954, when WRGB changed from Channel 4 to Channel 6, he was awarded the Medal of Honor by the Electronic Industry Association. He retired from GE in 1957 and died in 1960.

WORLD CHAMPIONS

Sports became a much bigger part of people's lives in the twentieth century and Schenectady was no exception.

The city's first world champion was a pocket billiards player by the name of Frank Taberski.

Born in 1889, Taberski won his first world title in 1917 and then held onto the championship for nine more challenge matches, at the time an unprecedented accomplishment. Taberski, who was known for his slow and deliberate style of play, used his fame to open a billiards hall and bowling center in Schenectady. He died in 1941.

Schenectadian Marty Servo won the world welterweight title in boxing when he knocked out Freddie "Red" Cochrane on February 1, 1946, in New York's Madison Square Garden. Servo was stopped in his next bout by middleweight champion Rocky Graziano on March 26. A broken nose in that bout effectively ended Servo's career and he fought only a few more times. He finished with a 48-4-2 record, two of those defeats coming at the hands of the great Sugar Ray Robinson.

Schenectady also produced a Little League World Series champion in 1954, while Pat Riley played basketball at Linton High and the University of Kentucky before embarking on a career in the National Basketball Association. He was a role player with the 1973 NBA Champion Los Angeles Lakers, and he coached both the Lakers and the Miami Heat to world titles.

Another homegrown product, Niskayuna's Jeff Blatnick, won the Olympic gold medal in wrestling at the 1984 Summer Olympics.

A LEGACY OF CHANGE

Henry Ford introduced the Model T in 1908, figured out how to mass produce it by 1913, and suddenly the automobile industry was booming. Joe Haraden, a native of Gouldsboro, Maine, and a recent graduate of the Massachusetts Institute of Technology, was working at the Schenectady General Electric plant as an engineer and saw an opportunity he couldn't pass up. In 1919, he decided a change in careers was in order.

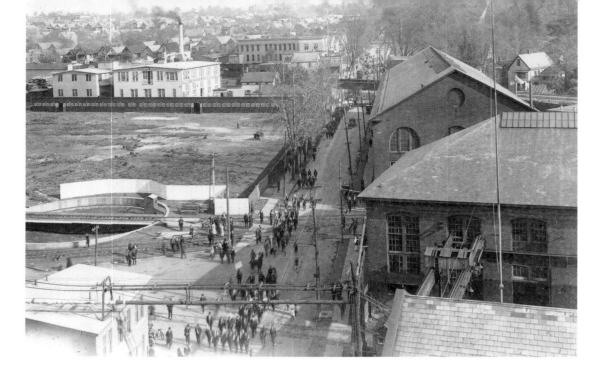

Right: ALCO Building.

Bottom, left: Horse-drawn carriages make their way down Dock Street, in 1902, passing in front of the General Electric Company.

Bottom, right: Joseph Haraden stands in the show room of Mohawk Auto on State Street in Schenectady around 1925.

Opposite page, top: General Electric employees.

Opposite page, Bottom: This photograph of GE's world-famous sign on top of Building 37 was taken between 1955-60.

Haraden had a few MIT classmates who had gone on to find success at General Motors, created in 1908, and perhaps with them in mind he decided to leave GE and open his own business selling cars on State Street Hill just up from what was then Crescent Park, now renamed Veterans Park.

Mohawk Auto Sales wasn't the first car dealership in Schenectady, but it's the only one that hasn't moved from its original location and has remained in the same family.

Haraden opted not to sell a Ford or a GM product and instead cast his lot with the Moon Motor Car Company, based in St. Louis. A car that was known for its quality and low costs, the Moon proved a popular product for many Americans in the first three decades of the 20th

century. The Company was created in 1905 by Joseph Moon and reached its peak in 1925, selling 10,271 automobiles.

According to the March 10, 1921, edition of the *Schenectady Gazette*, the automobile business was thriving. There were 7,979 cars registered in Schenectady County, an increase of nineteen percent from the previous year. Schenectadians, plagued by a number of trolley car strikes during that time, seemed ready to take to the road themselves.

Unfortunately, while the automobile industry was here to say, the same couldn't be said of the Moon Motor Car. The company's success began to fade quickly and by 1930 Moon, also hurt by the Great Depression, was out of the automobile business. Soon after that

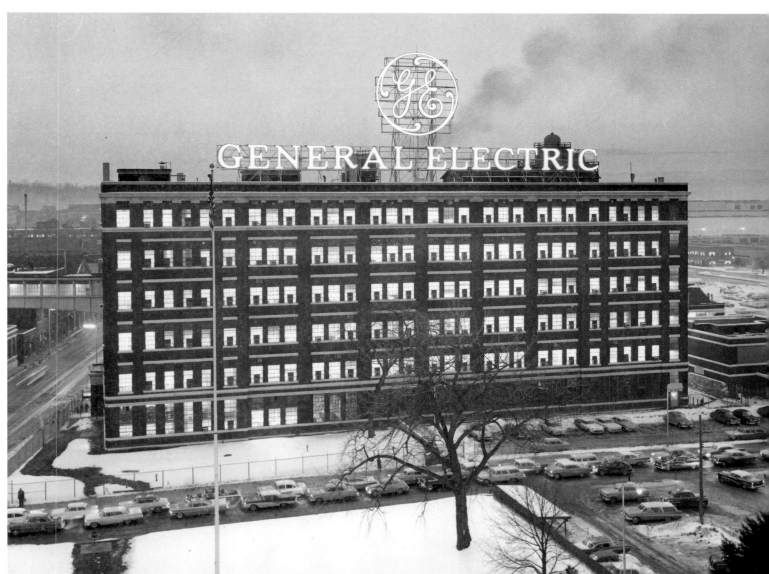

❖

Above: ALCO employees pose for this 1954 photograph standing next to the final tank produced by the plant.

Right: Sam Stratton poses for the camera in this 1959 photograph soon after being elected to the U.S. House of Representatives.

Mohawk Auto Sales became Mohawk Chevrolet. The company continued to sell Chevrolets until 1971 when the Haradens again changed their product and their name, this time becoming Mohawk Honda.

The 20th century marked a time of tremendous change for Schenectady. The city continued to grow eastward, away from the Mohawk River, and real estate magnate Henry Schermerhorn De Forest designed big houses and built them on beautiful avenues. A Republican, two-time mayor of the city (1885-87 and 89-91) and a U.S. Representative to Congress (1911-13), De Forest was a banker who became wealthy developing much of the area around Central Park.

Houses weren't the only things being built in Schenectady. Many new schools and parks were created in the first two decades, and the Western Gateway Bridge linking Schenectady to Scotia was built in 1925. In 1927 history touched down at the soon-to-be finished Schenectady County Airport, when Charles Lindbergh, fresh from his trip across the Atlantic Ocean, landed his plane before a large crowd.

Proctor's Theater was one of four new movie houses that popped up in downtown during the 1920s, and a new City Hall was completed in 1931, a year after Schenectady's population reached its all-time high of 95,692. The Great Depression hit Schenectady hard, as it did the rest of the country, but only one bank closed, and with the threat of war looming near the end

of the decade, GE and ALCO began to replenish their workforces. Schenectady's two biggest companies were major contributors to the war effort, but while World War II helped revive the nation's economy, the second half of the 20th century would not be a prosperous time for Schenectady.

The 1950s saw more schools being built to handle the post-war baby boom, and also emerging onto the scene was Sam Stratton. Born in Yonkers in 1916, Stratton and his family moved to Schenectady shortly after his birth, and then moved again, this time to Rochester, when Stratton was six.

After graduating from the University of Rochester and then earning a masters degree at both Haverford (1938) and Harvard (1940), Stratton spent a short time in Washington, D.C. working as an assistant for Democratic congressman Thomas Eliot. When war broke out, Stratton joined the U.S. Naval Reserve and served in the South Pacific until 1946.

Two years later Stratton came to Schenectady and, after lecturing for two years at Union College, embarked on a political career that he seemed well suited for. Using his charm and intelligence to win over voters, Stratton initially ran for City Council and won, and then in 1955 set his sights on the mayor's office, campaigning against rampant police corruption, and won that as well. Just two years later, in 1958, Stratton became only the second Schenectady Democrat

(George Lunn was the other) to earn a seat in the U.S. House of Representatives since the Civil War. He won 15 consecutive elections, most of them lopsided victories, and served in Congress for nearly 30 years before retiring in 1988 due to ill health. He died in 1990 just a few weeks shy of his eighty-fourth birthday.

The mayoral office in Schenectady passed back into Republican hands after Stratton exited for his long stint in Washington. Malcolm Ellis won three terms in the 1960s, and Frank Duci dominated the 1970s, winning in 1972, '76 and '80. But in the 1983 November election, a Democrat forced Duci to the sidelines as Karen Johnson became the city's first female mayor.

Born in Buffalo, raised in Cleveland, and educated at Radcliffe, Johnson moved to Schenectady in 1967 when her husband got a job at GE. After initially getting involved with the school board, Johnson won a seat on the City Council and then became its president. Her election to the mayor's office in 1983 prevented Duci from winning a fourth term, and she defeated him again in 1987. After eight years at the helm, much of the time dealing with a fizzling economy and downsizing at GE, Johnson decided not to run for a third term.

Duci became mayor for a fourth time in 1992, and was followed by fellow Republican Al Jurczynski for two terms beginning in 1996

and 2000. In 2004, the city's mayoral office returned to the Democrats—and the Stratton family—when Sam Stratton's son, Brian U. Stratton, began his first term. Stratton won a second term in the November 2007 election.

Although Schenectady hasn't recaptured its glory days of World War II when city streets were crowded with pedestrians day and night, it has experienced a substantial revival in the 21st century. Proctor's has brought national touring productions of Broadway shows to its expanded theater, new companies such as MVP Healthcare have moved into downtown, and a new movie theater, Bowtie Cinemas, has opened. GE remains an important presence in downtown, while in Niskayuna companies like the Knolls Atomic Power Laboratory and GE Global Research have helped Schenectady County continue to expand in the twenty-first century's first decade while most other upstate counties have declined in population.

❖

Clockwise from top:

Actor Richard Harris visited Schenectady's City Hall in 1983 and helped mayor Karen Johnson celebrate her birthday.

Karen Johnson was a member of the Schenectady City Council in 1976.

Pat Riley helped Jerry West and the Los Angeles Lakers to the 1973 NBA title.

Four-term Schenectady Mayor Frank Duci ran into his opponent Dave Roberts while both men were out trying to win votes during the 1978 election.

BIBLIOGRAPHY

Bowman, John S. *The Cambridge Dictionary of American Biography.* Cambridge University Press, Cambridge, G.B. (1995).

Bradley, James. *Before Albany: An Archaeology of Native Dutch Relations in the Capital Region.* New York State Museum (2007).

Brinkman, Lloyd M. *A History of Niskayuna, New York.* Niskayuna Historical Society (1976).

Brittain, J. E. *Electrical Engineering Hall of Fame.* Proc. of the IEEE. (2004).

Burke, Thomas E. *Mohawk Frontier: The Dutch Community of Schenectady, N.Y., 1661-1710.* Cornell University Press, Ithaca, N.Y. (1991).

Cornog, Evan. *The Birth of Empire: DeWitt Clinton and the American Experience, 1769-1828.* Oxford University Press, New York (1998).

Daily Union. "Those Who Gave." June 28, 1886.

Duanesburg Historical Society. *Images of America: Duanesburg and Princetown.* Arcadia Publishing, Charleston, S.C. (2005).

Dunn, Shirley. *The Mohicans and Their Land, 1609-1730.* Purple Mountain Press, Fleischmanns, N.Y. (1994).

Dunn, Walter S., Jr. *People of the American Frontier: The Coming of the Revolution.* Greenwood Publishing, Westwood, Ct. (2005).

Efner, William B. *The Public Life of Joseph C. Yates: Area Researchers and Writers Series. (1930-40).*

Featherstonhaugh, George W. "Schenectady and the Great Western Gateway: Past and Present," from Chapter IV: *"Canals and Railroads.* Schenectady County Chamber of Commerce (1926).

Guilderland Historical Society and Story House Corp. *Old Hellebergh.* Charlotteville, N.Y. (1975).

Halsey, Francis Whiting. *The Old New York Frontier.* Scribner & Sons, New York (1901).

Hanson, Willis T., Jr. *A History of Schenectady During the Revolution.* E. L. Hildreth, Brattleboro, Vt. (1916).

Hart, Larry. *Through the Darkest Hour.* Old Dorp Books, Scotia, N.Y. (1990).

Hendrickson, Kenneth E., Jr. *George R. Lunn and the Socialist Era in Schenectady, New York, 1909-1916.* New York History (1966).

Howell, G. R. and Munsell, J. H. *History of the County of Schenectady from 1662 to 1866.* W. W. Munsell & Co. Publishers, New York (1886)

Josephson, Matthew. *Edison: A Biography.* John Wiley & Sons, Inc. (1959).

Kobrin, David. *The Black Minority in New York.* The New York State Education Department (1971).

Larkin, Daniel F. *Pioneer American Railroads: The Mohawk and Hudson and the Saratoga and Schenectady Railroads.* Purple Mountain Press, Fleischmanns, N.Y. (1995).

Maston, Bruce. *An Enclave of Elegance: The GE Realty Plot.* Schenectady Museum, Schenectady (1984).

Neisuler, Jeanette G. *The History of Education in Schenectady, 1661-62 through 1961-62.* Board of Education, City School District, Schenectady (1964).

O'Toole, Fintan. *White Savage: William Johnson and the Invention of America.* Farrar, Straus and Girioux, New York (2005).

New York Times. "A Mohawk Town." Jan. 28, 1905.

Peckham, Howard H. *The Colonial Wars, 1689-1762.* The University of Chicago Press (1964).

Pearson, Jonathan. *A History of the Schenectady Patent in the Dutch and English Times.* Joel Munsell's Sons, Albany, N.Y. (1883).

Pearson, Jonathan and Griffis, William Elliot. *Three Centuries: The History of the First Reformed Church of Schenectady, 1680-1980.* Daily and Weekly Union, Steam Printing House, Schenectady (1880).

Rittner, Don. *Images of America: Schenectady's Stockade, New York's First Historic District.* Arcadia Publishing, Charleston, S.C. (2008).

Roberts, George S. *Old Schenectady.* Robson & Adee, Schenectady (1904).

Rosenthal, Susan. *Images of America: Schenectady.* Arcadia Publishing, Charleston, S.C. (1999).

Schenectady County Historical Society. *Images of America: Glenville.* Arcadia Publishing, Charleston, S.C. (2005).

Schenectady County Historical Society. *Images of America: Niskayuna.* Arcadia Publishing, Charleston, S.C. (2009).

Schenectady County Historical Society. *Images of America: Rotterdam.* Arcadia Publishing, Charleston, S.C. (2004).

Schenectady County Historical Society. *Images of America: Schenectady.* Arcadia Publishing, Charleston, S.C. (1999).

Schenectady County Sesquicentennial Historical Souvenir Program. *A Pair of Pioneers.* (1959).

Schenectady Gazette. "Moses Viney Obituary." Jan. 11, 1909.

Schenectady Gazette. "7,979 Motor Cars in Schenectady County." March 10, 1921.

Snow, Dean R. *The Iroquois.* Blackwell Publishers Inc., Cambridge, Mass. (2004).

Schenectady Union Star. "W.R.G. Baker Dies, GE Radio, TV Pioneer." Oct. 31, 1960.

Schenectady Union Star. April 4, 1961.

Staffa, Susan J. *Schenectady Genesis: How a Dutch Colonial Village Became an American City.* Purple Mountain Press, Fleischmanns, N.Y. (2004).

Steinbrenner, Richard T. *A Centennial Remembrance: The American Locomotive Company.* On Track Publishers, Inc., Warren, N.J. (2004).

Sullivan, James. *The History of New York State: 1523-1927.* Lewis Historical Publishing Company, New York and Chicago (1927).

Sullivan, James, editor. *Minutes of the Albany Committee of Correspondence, 1775-78, Schenectady Subcommittee.* University of the State of New York, Albany, N.Y. (1923).

Taormina, Frank. "Schenectady's Past." *Schenectady County Historical Society Newsletter.* (Jan.-Feb. 1996).

Van Buren, Martin. *"The Autobiography of Martin Van Buren.* Da Capo Press, New York (1920).

Van Epps, Percy M. *"The Van Epps Papers: A Collection of the Reports of Percy M. Van Epps on the History of the Town of Glenville.* Glenville Town Board (1998).

Winter, Kate H. *The Woman in the Mountain: Reconstruction of Self and Land by Adirondack Women Writers.* State University of New York Press, Albany, N.Y. (1989).

www.georgiaencyclopedia.org, *The New Georgia Encyclopedia.*

www.sewardhouse.org, *Seward House: A National Historic Landmark.*

Yates, Austin A. *Schenectady County, N.Y.: Its History to the Close of the Nineteenth Century.* New York History Company (1902).

Yetwin, Neil B. *Dr. Janet Murray, Schenectady's First Female Physician.* Schenectady County Historical Society Newsletter (March-April 2006).

The Spirit of Schenectady, a painting by Leonard Tantillo commissioned in 2006 to celebrate the seventy-fifth anniversary of Schenectady City Hall. The scene is as the artist imagines it to have looked when the building opened in 1931.

From left to right: Christopher Yates,
James Duane, Dirk Romeyn, Joseph
Yates, Charles Steinmetz, and
George Lunn.

ILLUSTRATIONS BY CARL BUELL.

SHARING THE HERITAGE

Historic profiles of businesses,
organizations, and families that have
contributed to the development and
economic base of Schenectady County

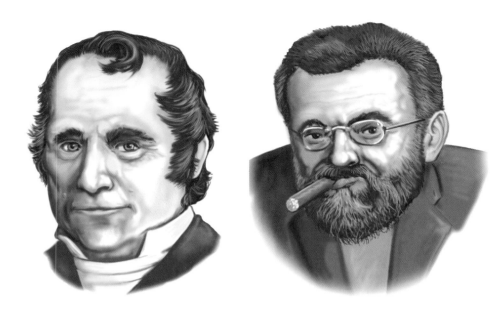

SCHENECTADY COUNTY HISTORICAL SOCIETY

❖

The founding of the Schenectady County Historical Society fulfilled the dream of the city's distinguished historian, Professor Jonathan Pearson of Union College, who noted in his journal in 1840 that:

"It is a thing much to be desired that some Schenectadian would 'endeavor' the history of this old town which has now been inhabited these more than two hundred years. Our ancients (sic) are passing away fast, family records and traditions are becoming scarce, and if the materials are not soon gathered, the beginnings of 'Old Dorp' [Schenectady] will be forgotten and unsung."

The Schenectady County Historical Society was established on July 14, 1905, under the Corporation Laws of the State of New York. The Society is an independent not-for-profit corporation, not a unit of government. Its stated mission as embodied in its constitution was, and remains, "to promote and encourage original historical research; to disseminate a greater knowledge of the history of the State of New York and particularly of Schenectady County; to gather, preserve, display, and make available for study artifacts, books, manuscripts, papers, photographs and other records and materials relating to the early and current history of Schenectady County and of the surrounding area; to encourage the suitable marking of places of historic interest; to acquire

Schenectady County Historical Society Building
11 Union Street

by purchase, gifts, devise, or otherwise the title to or the custody and control of historic sites and structures."

For seven years, the Society had no headquarters of its own, but was given space for exhibits in the Schenectady Public library. In December 1912, a committee responsible for finding a home for the Society succeeded in negotiating a three-year lease for the building at 11-13-15 Union Street that had been erected a half-century earlier to accommodate the offices of the County Clerk and the Surrogate and was no longer needed for that purpose. The exhibits were moved from the Library to the new home, and this became the location for monthly meetings for the next forty-six years.

In April 1958, the General Electric Company deeded to the Society the former G.E. Women's Club building at 32 Washington Avenue "as tangible evidence of its interest and desire to associate itself with those who are working to advance the city's cultural and educational activities." The Georgian style building, whose grounds are adjacent to the waters of the Binnekill and the Mohawk River, displays aspects of Federal and Greek Revival throughout the house. It is located in Schenectady's Stockade District, declared a national historic site in 1973. The building had been erected in 1895 by Jones Mumford Jackson as a home for himself

and his mother Dora, a widow, but both died within a few years of occupancy. An addition to the house was made in 1967, a meeting room named for local author John Vrooman. The Vrooman Room is also used periodically for museum exhibits.

A second major addition was added to the rear of the house in 1990. Called the Grems-Doolittle Library in honor of its major benefactor, Mandalay Grems, the Library and the Schenectady History Museum in the original house form the core of the Society's downtown Schenectady operations. In little over a decade, the 1990s, the Schenectady County Historical Society grew from a modest house museum called the Dora Jackson House with one room jammed with local history and genealogy, to the 12-room Schenectady History Museum; the adjoining Grems-Doolittle historical and genealogical library housing over 2,000 local family files, and the Mabee Farm Historic Site—three seventeenth-century farm buildings on nine acres in Rotterdam Junction, seven miles west of the City of Schenectady.

The Mabee homestead had been passed from generation to generation for 287 years before being deeded to the Society by George Franchere on January 29, 1993. Franchere also gave the Society 583 family papers including the deed passed by Daniel Van Antwerpen to Jan Mabee on January 29, 1705, and he provided generous financial support for Farm operations for several years after his initial gift. Mr. Franchere died in Florida in 2005 and is buried in Vale Cemetery. Dividends and interest from a trust fund that he established now provides the Society with a dependable annual income stream restricted to use at its Mabee Farm Historic Site. In accord with the Franchere will, part of that income was used in 2008 to purchase twenty-seven acres of adjacent land from Schenectady County, effectively quadrupling the size of the Farm.

Lack of proper office space and growing program activities at the Farm motivated the decision to build a year-round educational center at the Farm in memory of Mr. Franchere. The George E. Franchere Educational Center, to be build on part of the newly acquired land, will provide suitable car and bus parking; space for reception, presentation, and archaeological specimens; refreshment facilities; classrooms; and offices for Site management.

The Schenectady County Historical Society celebrated its Centennial in 2005, a half-century in the Stockade in 2008, and now, in 2009, it is celebrating the Bicentennial of Schenectady County through an extensive exhibit in its Vrooman Room and through the publication of Historic Schenectady County.

EDISON EXPLORATORIUM

Edison Exploratorium—Step into the past for a look at the future

In just seven years, the Edison Exploratorium has filled three huge buildings at 132, 134, and 136 Broadway in Schenectady with thousands of electrical age artifacts and archives. At first glance it resembles what an excited young engineering student called a great garage sale, but that same student spent hours examining it all. This stuff was the start, he proclaimed—and it all happened here.

The teenager's reaction was just what the Edison Exploratorium founders like to hear. It reflects our mission: In order to inform, inspire, and propel Schenectady into a brighter future, we will preserve, promote, and celebrate the unique heritage of Edison and the pioneers who gave birth to the Electric Age here in "The Original Electric City."

The Edison Exploratorium was chartered as a not-for-profit tax-exempt organization in June

A mural by artist Claude Seward displayed at the Edison Exploratorium. The mural celebrates the people and ideas that made Schenectady a pioneering center in the electrical age. Edison and Steinmetz are at bottom right. The electrical pioneers whose images surround the young Edison are (clockwise from top, center) Irving Langmuir, Charles Curtis, Elihu Thomson, William Coolidge, Willis Whitney, Christian Steenstrup, Frank Sprague, and Ernst Alexanderson.

2001 with directors Thurston Sack as president, James Delmonaco as vice president, and John Harnden as secretary/treasurer.

The Exploratorium serves as a workshop for those interested in seeing how technological advances have evolved. Its programs have attracted scientists, engineers, and others from around the globe, student groups from the area, as well as GE's Edison Engineering program, interns, and co-ops. Visitors find that, here in Schenectady, the spirit of Edison is alive.

The Edison Exploratorium is just a start but it is growing and we are interested in building a world-class facility. We need to gather our rich heritage that organizations like the GE Elfun Society saved in order to preserve the electrical history that emerged in Schenectady. Millions of photographs, films, and rare archives are at the Hall of Electrical History at the Schenectady Museum. Hundreds of other industrial and electrical age artifacts are located at Union College, the city's Efner museum, and the Schenectady County Historical Society. The artifacts illustrate the technologies of recording, broadcasting, transportation (air, land and sea), lighting, medical, power generation, and consumer products. Presently, the Exploratorium is utilizing its extensive website, a virtual public space which individuals can access regardless of physical location and can interact. It is a place where people can meet, exchange ideas, share technical information, provide support, and discuss global concerns, such as how technology can address future energy needs.

We invite you to see how the Edison Exploratorium has grown. Not only are its thousands of artifacts and interactive displays serving students as building blocks to expand technology ever further today, but other programs are spurring interest in technology. For example, a video project, "Wizards of Schenectady: Chronicling the Past, Building the Present, Imagining the Future", is well underway, led by Mike Whalen, the resident expert behind the camera at the Edison Exploratorium. He is capturing the heritage of Schenectady County's Tech Valley from the unique perspective of those who knew and know past and current technological inventors and entrepreneurs. By standing on the shoulders of these giants, we can build a better future.

The Edison Exploratorium.

Schenectady was ready for business when Edison arrived in 1886. During colonial days, Schenectady thrived as the gateway to the west with industries like boat building and broom corn manufacturing. Later came steam-driven farm machinery and locomotives. Then Thomas Edison arrived in 1886 to occupy two vacant locomotive buildings and to earn Schenectady the title of "The city that Lights and Hauls the World."

Behind it all were business and community leaders who knew and embraced the value of progress. It didn't just begin with enticing Edison to come to Schenectady with a site ready for production and financial incentives.

The boat-building industry resulted from careful exploring by Arendt Van Curler who realized Schenectady was the place where the river had many islands with only a few rapids to the west, an ideal place for trade. To avoid the Cohoes falls, people would come by stagecoach from Albany and then head west after buying Schenectady and Durham boats. In 1790 Philip Schuyler convinced state lawmakers to support the Western Inland Navigation Company. This was followed by DeWitt Clinton's involvement in getting the federal government to support the Erie Canal, which opened in 1825.

Later in the 1800s, Schenectady County was the broom capital of the world. Broom corn, a type of grass with stiff bristles instead of corn ears, was introduced by the Shakers of Watervliet and Niskayuna. Many of Schenectady's patroons

got their start raising broom corn. An acre produced enough for some 250 brooms. Key among these was William Schermerhorn, who also became one of the largest manufacturers of brooms in the United States.

It was business foresight that brought Schenectady fame as a locomotive center. George W. Featherstonhaugh, who built the first line to connect the Mohawk River with the Hudson, made history when the historic steam locomotive *DeWitt Clinton* came into Schenectady on August 13, 1831. John Ellis and Platt Potter sought the Norris brothers of Philadelphia who knew how to build locomotives. On January 15, 1848, a total of $40,000 was raised in Schenectady. With Norris contributing $10,756 in tools and machinery the Schenectady Locomotive Engine Manufactory was born, headed up by Ellis, Potter, Daniel Campbell, J..C. Wright, and John Ellis. Joining them was Chief Engineer Walter McQueen, whose reputation earned the locomotives the title of "McQueen Engines." The business took off after the Civil War when the 226 locomotive, which could go 82 miles in 83 minutes, was introduced. In 1880, the Pitkin-designed 440 engine became the most popular locomotive as the rails went west. It was during these booming years that seven companies merged to form the American Locomotive Company (ALCO). In 1907, 6200 workers built 942 locomotives.

Another key business for Schenectady came with the arrival of George Westinghouse in 1856 to manufacture farm implements, including the first steam-driven grain and clover threshing machine. A holder of seven patents, his "G. Westinghouse & Co." was the market leader in labor saving devices for the farmer. The company sign stood along the Edison Works and later General Electric until 1922. A missed opportunity occurred when his young son, George Jr., who did sales work for his father by train, came up with a device for replacing derailed cars. A financing plan in Schenectady did not work, so young George Westinghouse, Jr., went to Pittsburgh to find investors who shared his interest—an interest that led George, at age twenty-two, to become president of the Westinghouse Air Brake Company in 1869. This led to the formation of Westinghouse Electric in 1886 to compete with Thomas Edison. Ironically, the old farm machinery site along the Erie Canal was later absorbed into GE and it was there that radio and television was developed.

The year 1886 was pivotal for Schenectady, too. Thomas Edison, a successful entrepreneur in the infant electrical industry, began looking for a site to which to move his machine works from New York. Edison needed an immediate manufacturing site and liked the two unused McQueen locomotive buildings by the Mohawk River. Edison was already familiar with Schenectady having received an honorary degree from Union College. Edison made an offer but it was $7,500 below what the owners wanted, so Schenectadians raised the money to make the sale.

In the summer of l886 the work of moving the machine shop began and three years later the Edison Machine Works became part of the Edison Electric Company. Another three years and the Edison General Electric and Thomson Houston Company were united to become the General Electric Company.

Of all the outstanding scientists and engineers, there was one that indisputably became the most revered—Charles Proteus Steinmetz. This mathematical genius stood just 4'3" tall. But he was a mental giant in understanding how electricity worked, starting with his law of hysteresis. To hire him in l892, GE had to buy the hatmaking firm he worked for in Yonkers. Hailed worldwide as the "forger of thunderbolts," he created an artificial 120,000-volt lightning machine as part of his studies to increase the reliability of electric power transmission.

While Edison had over 1,000 U.S. Patents, primarily for products such as the incandescent lamp and phonograph, compared to over 200 for Steinmetz, mainly for production, generation, and distribution of electricity, it was

electrical engineers all over the world who sought Steinmetz out to solve problems, referring to him as the Supreme Court. He freely shared his ideas. Henry Ford unofficially came to Schenectady for advice on putting headlights on his cars, but not without Steinmetz asking him to contribute to schools in Detroit, which he did.

(Steinmetz's Camp Mohawk was moved to the Henry Ford Museum in Michigan). Steinmetz also became a part-time professor at Union College from 1902 to 1923; the engineering building there now bears his name. He also headed up the American Institute of Electrical Engineers, without compensation. "It's not work if it interests you," he once said as he shared his ideas and solved problems for anyone who asked. Deciding not to marry and have children, he adopted the entire Hayden family who lived with him on Wendell Avenue where he invited children in to see his greenhouse collections, including exotic animals. Midge, his granddaughter who recently died, told many stories of how he freely gave away money when people came to the door with the philosophy that, yes some may not really need it but think of those who really do. Well known for his sense of humor, he used to invite the ladies to look at themselves in a mirror lit by a vapor lamp that made people appear blue before he figured out how to eliminate that defect. The electrical

Today, the County of Schenectady has the original Certificate Changing Place of Business *of the Edison Machine Works signed by Samuel Insull, John Kruesi, Charles Batchelor, Henry Livor, and Thomas A. Edison. Schenectady businessmen were short just $500 the day $7500 was due to Edison. Col. Bob Furman, a member of the state legislature, was sitting outside the closed Mohawk Bank, thinking the task hopeless, when Jonathan Levi, from the grocery store next door, offered to give half if Furman would give the other half. They roused W. G. Schermerhorn, an officer in the bank who was still inside, and he agreed to grant the $500 note. A telegram was immediately sent to De Remer, a Schenectady attorney in New York, and he closed the deal with minutes to spare.*

HISTORICALGESIGN1886

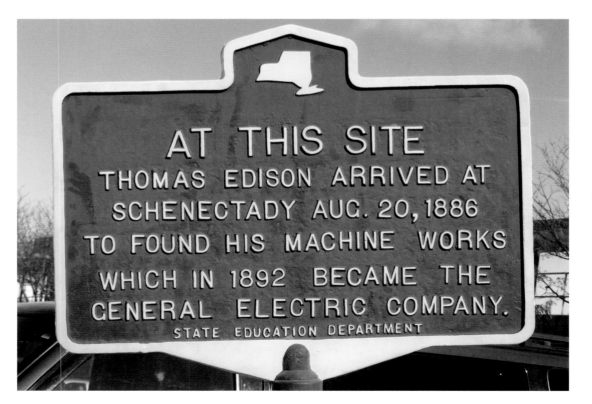

AT THIS SITE
THOMAS EDISON ARRIVED AT
SCHENECTADY AUG. 20, 1886
TO FOUND HIS MACHINE WORKS
WHICH IN 1892 BECAME THE
GENERAL ELECTRIC COMPANY.
STATE EDUCATION DEPARTMENT

❖

In just two years, GE engineers revolutionized power generation by introducing GE's first 5000kw vertical shaft steam turbine. It was built for the Chicago Edison Company in l903. Technology moved so fast that this pioneering turbine was soon replaced. But it was not forgotten; it was brought back as a monument. At the dedication service are (from left to right) E. W. Rice, W. L. Emmet, Edison, George Morrison, Steinmetz, H.F. T. Erben, and an unidentified mailboy.

#118592

wizard was revered by Schenectadians, including thousands of immigrants arriving each year to find jobs at the Schenectady Works. The city of Schenectady named a school and a park after him because of his civic contributions. He was best known for running for school board with a platform of "A seat for every child."

Since the Edison and Steinmetz eras, there have been ups and downs in business in Schenectady. World War II reached a high of 45,000 employees, with some 359 buildings covering 677 acres, at times called a city within a city. One consistent trend paving the way for growth has been engineering and research, much of it still performed in Schenectady where the first in the US Industrial Research Lab was created by GE, first as

a lab in the Steinmetz barn on Erie Boulevard and then formally with Dr. Willis Whitney as director. Technological advances developed in Schenectady have spawned business growth throughout the world. During the Edison and Steinmetz Eras, the electrical age came into full swing with firsts in generation and transmission, starting with Curtis and Emmet's two horizontal shaft steam turbines of 500 and l500kw in l901.

After 1903, there was no stopping the electrification of the world, be it in the home, or for land, air, and sea transportation, for military, industrial and agricultural applications as well as for the communications, medical, and entertainment businesses. At one time, after GE Board Chairman Cordiner decentralized the company, more than

150 manufacturing plants in the U.S. could trace their beginning to Schenectady-invented products. A popular one was the Monitor-Top refrigerator, engineered by Christian Steenstrup, which was first produced here and got its name from the Clute Foundry in Schenectady which produced the gun turret for the north's Civil War *Monitor* ship, a turret that resembled the hermetically sealed top of the GE refrigerator.

On the shoulders of these electrical giants to bring us into the electronic age came Ernst Alexanderson, Irving Langmuir, and William Coolidge. GE was no stranger to wireless technology. The company's co-founder with Edison, Thomson had sent wireless signals one hundred feet in 1875. But it was Dr. Alexanderson who revolutionized radio communication with his alternator. The first one now is in the Smithsonian Institute. .

There were still some problems with amplification and it was Langmuir with his pliotron vacuum tube that solved this problem. Langmuir went on to win the Nobel Prize in 1932 for surface chemistry. The world became familiar with radio as news and entertainment when WGY in 1922 broadcast its first radio drama, "The Wolf."

With the outbreak of World War II, GE converted its electronic technology to wartime needs, particularly in developing over sixty types of radar systems. Enhancing Langmuir's work with vacuum tube development were Albert Hull, William White, and Saul Dushman. Coolidge became world famous for developing a ductile tungsten process which revolutionized electric lighting, and also led to the modern type of x-ray tube. That x-ray business evolved into advanced computerized tomography and MRI, medical advances being further developed today at GE Global Research. In 1960, Ivar Giaever's discovery of super-conductive tunneling led to his award, in 1973, of a Nobel Prize for physics.

A few of the major "firsts" developed in Schenectady:

- The first practical large-scale turbine with concave buckets;
- The first commercial electric locomotive;
- The first use of ductile tungsten for electric lights;
- The first hermetically sealed "Monitor Top" refrigerator;

- The first large-screen demonstration of TV at Proctor's;
- The first televised news event (Al Smith accepts the presidential nomination in 1928);
- The first man-made diamonds;
- The first microwave tube;
- The first saturable reactor animated controlled display sign;
- The first use of amplidynes for radar and industrial controls;
- The first use of computerized tomography, MRI, and digital imaging;
- Ship propulsion systems;
- The first "talking" moving picture;
- The first television relay;
- The first large AC & DC motors;
- The largest steel mill motor;
- The first voice communication to the moon;
- The first X-ray tube and medical electronics
- The first coast-to-coast facsimile transmission;
- The first cloud seeding
- The first laser diode
- The first defect-free silicon

GE continues its leadership role in research innovations to meet today's needs, particularly in alternative energy programs. A new and growing wind generator engineering center at Schenectady is a natural evolution of the birth of power generation technology here. So it is with great pride that we at the Edison Exploratorium invite the next generation of entrepreneurs to step into the past for a better look at the future.

By working together, we can once again make Schenectady the place to be.

Dr. Alexanderson's dream of adding sight to radio was realized in 1926 when he developed a mechanical scanning disc system for television. A live vaudeville show from the Bldg. 36 "studio" was transmitted to Proctor's theater on May 22, 1930. This first public TV transmission demonstration was viewed by science writers from all over the world.

#442856

ELLIS MEDICINE

BELLEVUE WOMAN'S CENTER

ELLIS HOSPITAL

McCLELLAN CAMPUS

NEW CITY HOSPITAL
6106 Schenectady, N.Y.

Above: Ellis Hospital, construction nearly complete in 1906 at corner of Nott Street and Rosa Road. The hospital was previously located on Jay Street from 1893-1906 and was preceded by its forerunner, the Schenectady Free Dispensary which opened on Christmas Day, 1885 on lower Union Street.

Below: Ellis Hospital, Nott Street, 2008.

Opposite, top: Nurses tend to newborns in the nursery at Bellevue Woman's Hospital in earlier years.

Opposite, bottom: Surgery at St. Clare's Hospital in the 1950s.

Ellis has long provided the highest quality of care for residents of the Capital Region. Established in 1885 as the Schenectady Free Dispensary, Ellis has grown and continued to adapt to the ever-changing needs of the community it serves. The five-bed ward served as the city's first medical facility at a time when the population topped 13,000 and was in dire need of an infirmary. It also marked the beginning of a time-honored tradition of hospital and community working together to make healthcare an enduring priority. Little did the founders of Ellis Hospital know that their humble beginnings would positively impact so many lives, for so many generations.

The hospital was established through the charitable support of the community, along with the generosity of Charles G. Ellis who contributed $25,000 towards the construction of the initial facility. His donation was given in honor of his father, John Ellis, founder of Schenectady Locomotive Works and namesake of Ellis Hospital. Building upon the "benevolence of the people" and a commitment to superior healthcare, Ellis Hospital has continued to flourish through the years. Today, Ellis' mission is resolute: to meet the healthcare needs of its community with excellence. The organization's vision is rooted in its steadfast commitment to ensure continued access to a full range of quality healthcare services in its community.

Today, Ellis Medicine, the new umbrella name for the entire organization, is in the midst of reconfiguring healthcare in Schenectady as part of statewide hospital reforms mandated by New York

State law. As the sole provider of acute hospital care in Schenectady County, Ellis is proud to carry on the traditions of the former Bellevue Woman's Hospital and the former St. Clare's Hospital as a single, stronger, and unified healthcare organization. Indeed, the legacies of Bellevue and St. Clare's are an inextricable part of Ellis' contemporary history.

The former Bellevue Woman's Hospital, now known as Bellevue Woman's Center (a service of Ellis Medicine), was founded in 1931 by Mary Grace Jorgensen, a twenty-eight-year-old nurse and mother of two. She was a visionary in an era when women gave birth at home. She envisioned a facility offering care for the particular needs of women, their babies and their families. Throughout its years of providing care to women and infants, Bellevue has seen numerous medical pioneers come through its doors, including Dr. Virginia Apgar, who designed and introduced the Apgar score for newborns, and Dr. T. Berry Brazelton, an acclaimed child development specialist.

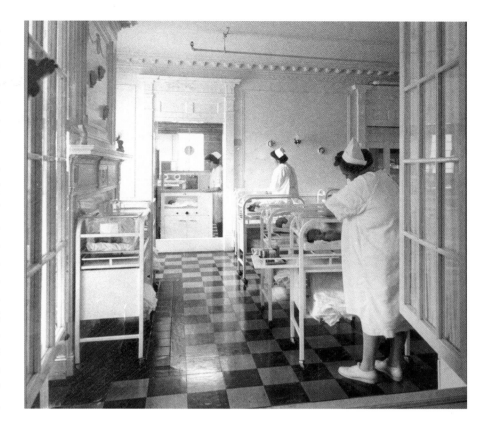

Today, Bellevue continues Mary Grace Jorgensen's dedication to women's healthcare needs by providing a unique depth and breadth of services for women in every stage of their life. Bellevue is renowned for unsurpassed care, with its expert physicians and nurses and the largest obstetrical services in Northeastern New York. From maternity services, advanced diagnostic breast care center and pelvic health center to surgical services, diagnostic imaging and community education, Bellevue provides quality care in the most comfortable of settings. In 2006, Bellevue welcomed its 110,000th baby to be born at the hospital, surpassing all others in the Capital Region. Bellevue also has the only high-risk neonatal center in Schenectady County and one of only three in the entire region. In addition, Bellevue's mobile mammography outreach program serves twelve counties and reaches over 1,200 underserved women annually.

The caring tradition of the former St. Clare's Hospital is also carried on by Ellis Medicine, including the important role of providing care to disadvantaged members of the community. The public movement that created St. Clare's stretches back to the early 1940s when Barney Fowler, an acclaimed area journalist, and Frank Dickershaid, a retired roofing contractor, visited the offices of

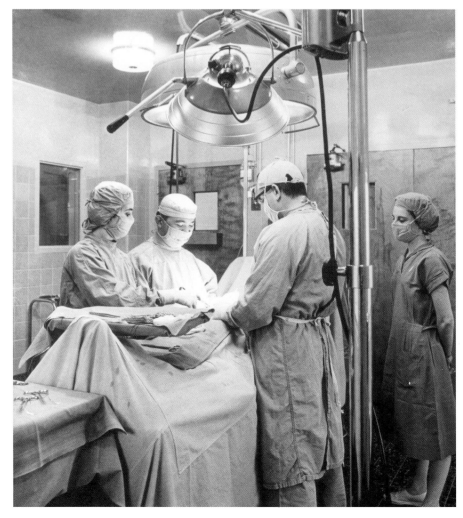

Albany's Bishop Edmund Gibbons. They were informed that they would need petitions with a minimum of 20,000 signatures to establish the required interest in such an undertaking. Six weeks later they had gathered 25,000 signatures. Seven years later, in September of 1949, the doors of St. Clare's Hospital finally opened under the guidance of the Albany Catholic Diocese and the Franciscan Sisters of the Poor. The following is one of the more cherished descriptions of the hospital. "These buildings do not rest upon a foundation of cement and sand but upon the solid rock of love and faith. Its corridors are filled with whispered prayers. There is a soft and tranquil beauty in its pastel colored walls and the hush of peace about its business of healing."

Today, Ellis' McClellan campus (formerly St. Clare's) is home to an array of quality outpatient services, including day surgery, medical imaging, primary, pediatric and dental care, laboratory services, infusion therapy, physical therapy, a wound care program, and a sleep disorders center, as well as a full-service emergency department that operates 24/7, and is the community's "medical home."

As a 455-bed community and teaching hospital, Ellis moves forward in its history having successfully combined Schenectady's three great hospital traditions into one, unified organization. Ellis provides a broad scope of quality services on three campuses—Bellevue Woman's Center, Ellis Hospital, and Ellis'

McClellan Campus—ranging from emergency, medical/surgical, mental health and cancer care, to maternity/women's health, primary care, long-term care and outpatient services. Ellis is nationally recognized for patient safety, clinical excellence, and for its quality stroke, bariatric (weight loss surgery), and cardiac care. Ellis is one of only three programs in the Capital Region authorized to perform cardiac surgery and its cardiac catheterization laboratory is one of the busiest in the area. Ellis Medicine is also the sponsor of the respected Ellis Hospital School of Nursing, and Family Medicine Residency and Dental Residency programs, which strengthen our communities by providing talented new healthcare professionals.

By incorporating state-of-the-art technology and advanced medical procedures with the traditional art of caring and a steadfast commitment to provide the highest quality of care to each patient, Ellis has continued to build on its reputation as a trusted source of healthcare in the region. The organization, with more than 3,400 employees and more than 600 physicians and dentists with privileges, is also one of the largest employers in the Capital Region.

Going forward, the goal of Ellis Medicine is to create a stronger, more effective health care delivery system for the communities it serves. The organization's long-term plan includes: constructing a new, larger, state-of-the-art emergency department at Ellis Hospital; enhancing women's and infant's services at Bellevue; re-locating Ellis' nursing home from the hospital to the campus on McClellan Street for an improved setting for patients and families; developing a "medical home" at the McClellan campus that improves access to primary care and preventive/wellness medicine; plus there are plans to extend Ellis' emergency services to Southern Saratoga County, one of the region's fastest growing communities.

Ellis Medicine stands at the beginning of a new era of healthcare in Schenectady, with the strength that comes with uniting the community's three great hospital traditions and the untold promise of what is possible moving forward, together. For more information about Ellis and what the organization has to offer, please visit www.ellismedicine.org.

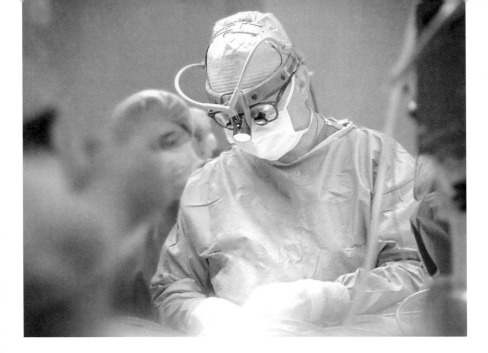

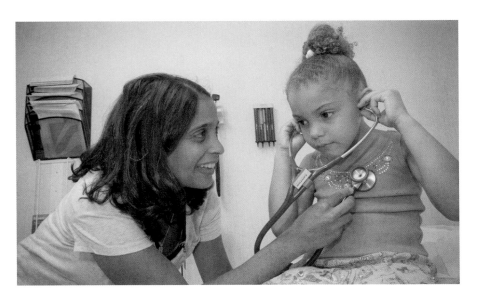

UNION COLLEGE

Union College has a long, rich history, offering a legacy to the alumnus that is rare among its competition. Chartered in 1795, it is one of the oldest colleges in New York, second only to Columbia University.

The growing excitement of becoming a new nation swelled throughout the burgeoning colonies after Burgoyne's defeat at Saratoga during the American Revolutionary War, prompting several hundred residents of northern New York to demand a means of higher education. For sixteen years, academic and clerical activists made their demands known, resulting in the recognition of the school by the Regents of the State of New York with the state's first charter in 1795. On September 30, 1795, the Union College Board enrolled twenty-three students in the new college.

The name, Union College, represented the very essence of what the founding fathers recognized as the heart of the new college. Several differing religious and national groups with a spirit of cooperation were instrumental in the formation of the college. The founders were adamantly against the separatist characteristics of preceding American colleges in religion and academics evidenced by Union's motto, "We all become brothers under the laws of Minerva." Union is now one of the oldest

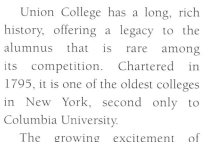
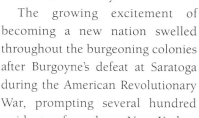

Above: An aerial view of Union College campus.

Below: Chester Arthur Memorial on Union campus—one of the few U.S. presidents to serve without being elected. He took office after President James Garfield was assassinated in 1881. Union College was his alma mater.

nondenominational colleges in the country and was among the first to offer French on an equal plain with Greek and Latin.

Union College deviated from the classical curriculum that was most widely accepted during the early nineteenth century. Under the direction of Eliphalet Nott, President of Union College from 1804 to 1866, the college began a new "scientific course" of study with a considerable emphasis on natural history, science, modern languages, and mathematics. Although Nott was looked upon by his peers with bewilderment, his more practical approach to courses of study offered at Union eventually gained acceptance. During this time, the College's annual fee was $55.50, which covered tuition, room, board, and stove, and the use of books, firewood, and candles.

Because of Nott's willingness to stray from the "traditional," Union became the first liberal arts college to offer engineering in 1845. It was also one of the first to include in its studies American history and constitutional government, along with pioneering an elective system of study.

Nott was also creative in his approach to investment methods. His solution to bring Union College into financial solvency involved instituting a statewide lottery. Clearing his first hurdle, convincing the Union trustees, he lobbied the Legislature and won their approval. With the proceeds from the lottery, Nott purchased 250 acres of land on the edge of town for the future college campus. He procured a French architect, Joseph Ramée, to design a campus that would compete with the well established colleges at that time; Harvard, Princeton, Yale, Brown, and Rutgers.

Ramée envisioned a campus with a round, domed building in the center, surrounded by dormitories, classrooms, and open space. A sixteen-sided building in the center of the campus, standing 102 feet high at the pinnacle, was designed by Edward Tuckerman Potter, Nott's grandson and a Union College graduate. Construction began on the building in 1858, then called the Alumni or Graduates' Hall, but was not officially completed until 1879. The idiosyncratic campus centerpiece incorporates manifold aspects from both religion and rationalism, symbolizing a unified aggregation apropos for a college called "Union."

It was not until 1904, on the centennial of Nott's inauguration as Union's president, when the college dedicated the building in his honor, renaming it the "Nott Memorial." Today it is a National Historic Landmark and a center for lectures, conferences, exhibits, and study.

During the presidency of Andrew Van Vranken Raymond, 1894 to 1907, the College saw a resurgence in enrollment. Among Raymond's successful innovations was the establishment of a Department of Electrical Engineering and Applied Physics. His choice to head up the department was as ingenious as establishing the department itself. Charles P. Steinmetz, the "electrical wizard" of the General Electric Company, was appointed as department head,

captivating the attention of many new applicants and breathing life into the struggling college.

Today, Union is ranked among the top liberal arts colleges in America and is widely regarded for its academic excellence. It continues to "think out of the box" with its work in

Above: The "Dutchmen" Union College hockey team.

Below: The gateway to the Union College campus.

interdepartmental studies cutting across the lines of academic disciplines. Interdepartmental majors are available in multifarious areas, along with programs designed to enable students to work toward both a bachelor's degree and an advanced degree.

Its list of graduates through the years resembles a "Who's Who." Among this alumni

list is the father of Franklin D. Roosevelt, the grandfather of Winston Churchill, a United States President (Chester A. Arthur), 15 United States senators, 91 members of the House of Representatives, 13 governors, 7 cabinet secretaries, 50 prominent diplomats, over 200 judges, 40 missionaries, 16 generals, and 90 college presidents, including the first presidents of the University of Illinois, the University of Iowa, the University of Michigan, and Vassar College.

In Union College's endeavor to "blur the lines between life inside and outside the classroom," they established the Minerva House System (named for the Roman Goddess of wisdom who appears on the College's shield). In recent years, many old fraternity houses were acquired by the College in order to create the System. Seven houses were renovated in 2004, creating The Minervas, in an attempt to "broaden the educational experience" beyond the classroom, with each incoming freshman randomly affiliated with one of the houses for the duration of their stay at Union.

Each Minerva House has its own yearly entertainment budget, and plans events and activities for its members from friendly competitions to showing movies or hosting "CrossTalks." They are each led by a faculty and student representative in their own governing

council, and have become the link in communicating both large and small ideas throughout the campus.

Union College is referred to as the "Mother of Fraternities." More fraternities have been formed at Union than any other college or university, including the first three in America. The "Union Triad" is a name given to the first three Greek letter social fraternities with a continuing record. They were the Kappa Alpha Society (1825), the oldest fraternity in the nation, the Sigma Phi Society (1827), and Delta Phi (1827). Sigma Phi is the only one that remains, making it the oldest fraternity chapter in the nation.

The lovely 120-acre campus includes eight acres of formal gardens and woodland known as Jackson's Garden. In 1973, the hit movie, The Way We Were, starring Robert Redford and Barbara Streisand, was filmed at the College, using many students as extras.

Union is at home in Schenectady, offering tremendous educational and cultural opportunities to the community, whether through free lectures and exhibits at the Nott Memorial, plays at the Yulman Theater, or the popular, affordable chamber concerts in Memorial Chapel. In addition, downtown businesses depend on the College's 840 employees and 2,150 students and their families

to help their establishments thrive. Through the Union Schenectady Initiative, the College has invested more than $10 million to renovate dozens of homes, transform the streetscape, and enhance the safety of surrounding neighborhoods.

For additional information, please visit www.union.edu.

Above: Students on the picturesque Union Campus.

Below: Students enjoying a spring day on the Union campus.

PRICE CHOPPER-GOLUB CORPORATION

The story of Price Chopper Supermarkets is a story of the true American dream. Russian immigrant, Lewis Golub, arrived on the shores of America in 1900, bringing with him his wife, Tillie, and the dream of financial success in a country where dreams can come true.

During this time, Lewis set in motion what today is an extremely successful supermarket chain, with his first business, a lunchroom that operated until 1907. From there he opened a small dairy store which eventually turned into a wholesale grocery business. Lewis along with

his wife and children, Dorothy, Bernard, and William, invested long hours in the family business. Through their tenacity and strong work ethic, despite the odds, the company soon grew large enough to expand into a rented warehouse. But this was only to be the tip of the iceberg for the Golub family.

Both Golub sons matriculated at Union College and went on to earn degrees; Bernard (Ben), from Columbia University in 1925, and William (Bill), from University of Michigan in 1926, thus entering the business arena with youthful energy and renewed objectives. Shortly before his passing in 1930, Lewis merged his company with fellow entrepreneur Joseph Grosberg's company, creating a larger, stronger wholesale grocery firm as his legacy to his sons.

By November 1932, Ben and Bill launched into uncharted territory with the area's first "one-stop shopping" market in Green Island, New York. The "Public Service Market," as it was named, was the early forerunner of modern supermarkets. They were truly entrepreneurs and pioneers in a brand new business. This innovative store, even in those dark times in America's history, was a success; so much so that the Golub brothers opened a second market in Watervliet, New York, just a few months later. The Public Service Markets offered everything from groceries, fresh produce, and dry goods, to clothing, a barber shop and a cafeteria, all conveniently located under one roof.

In 1935 the Golubs moved to Schenectady and opened the first Central Markets located near Central Park.

During 1943, the Golub family became sole owners of the Central Markets when they bought out Grosberg and formed the present Golub Corporation. In the following years the Golubs, known for their innovation, had many "firsts" in the industry. In 1951, Central Markets became one of the first grocery chains in the country to offer S & H Green Stamps. During that same year, Central Markets, in order to lend a hand to the local agricultural industry, aided in the formation of the Empire State Red Label Egg Program, ensuring fresh eggs to their patrons and offering a guarantee to purchase farmers crops at fair market prices.

In 1958, Bill initiated a program involving 4-H participants, offering free seeds under the agreement that the company would buy back the best of the young farmers' crops for resale at Central Market stores. In the 1960s, they added a number of new stores (North Adams, Mechanicville, Oneonta, Glens Falls and Saratoga).

In 1973, in yet another industry leading concept, all Central Market locations opened their doors twenty-four hours per day, seven days a week. "The whole idea is to better service customers…we are always here when you need us. When you need something, no matter what the hour, you will be able to get it at Central Markets," said Neil Golub at the time. After Ben passed away in 1972, the Golub Corporation adopted a new name in 1974, Price Chopper, to reflect their new pricing policy offering the area's competitive low price, high quality guarantee.

By the 1970s, another Golub generation took the reins. Lewis and Neil became the third generation of Golubs to carry the Price Chopper torch. By this time Price Chopper had already

Opposite, top: The Central Market Bellevue branch in the 1930s.

Opposite, left: Lewis Golub I, he was born in Russia and came to America in 1900.

Opposite, bottom: The railroad company photo depicts the trolley cars that were running until 1925. Buses were used after 1946. The building was sold in 1951, it became Price Chopper market in 1976. The Golub Family built the Eastern Parkway store that exists today in 1993. This is the significance of the photo as it relates to Price Chopper.

Below: (From left to right) Jerry Golub, David Golub, Lewis Golub, Neil Golub, and Mona Golub.

Above: A Price Chopper supercenter at Mohawk Commons in Niskayuna at its grand opening in March of 2002. An adjoining Marshalls department store can be seen in the upper right corner.

Below: This mid-size Price Chopper supermarket on Altamont Avenue in the Town of Rotterdam anchored a small shopping plaza. The plaza still stands without the market, which was replaced in 2003 by a new Price Chopper supercenter a short distance away. Each of Schenectady County's three largest towns, Rotterdam, Glenville, and Niskayuna, now has a supercenter.

expanded into Massachusetts, Utica and Syracuse, New York. In the early 1990s, the company expanded to Vermont, Worcester, Massachusetts, and New Hampshire.

Price Chopper's tag line, "We're Not Just In Your Neighborhood, We're Your Neighbor" has defined their commitment to discovering the most beneficial ways to serve their patrons and the communities they live in. The Golubs are proud that more than 10,000 charitable and philanthropic organizations have benefited from the company's financial support and involvement through company programs and the volunteer time of Price Chopper associates.

One such program, "Making Strides Against Breast Cancer," is one that is particularly close to the hearts of the Price Chopper family. On

April, 3, 2007, dear friend and valued associate, thirty-eight year-old Laura Gismondi, lost her battle with breast cancer. Because of Laura and thousands of others in Price Chopper's communities, Price Chopper is more dedicated than ever to ending this deadly disease. They have incorporated in-store sales, and marketing programs to raise funds and awareness such as bake sales, spare change collections, and participation on the Price Chopper walk team.

Neil and Lewis redefined Price Chopper in the 1990s with a bold effort to make the company a premiere retailer and the "Best in Fresh." In 1997, Price Chopper was among the first supermarkets on the Internet at www.pricechopper.com. Today, its award-winning website features their weekly specials, recipes, and the ability to order party platters, and send flowers through FTD.

Over the years much has changed, and yet, some things remain. Bill died in 1992. A new generation of Golubs joined the leadership, and Price Chopper grew to over 116 locations in six states by 2007, continuing to flow with the ever-changing tide of progress. What has remained is the Golubs' dedication to serve their loyal customers, regard their workforce as "family" and give back to the community that has given them so much.

G & M Auto Tech began as G & M Affiliates over fifty years ago in 1954, with Bob Garbellano's father, Ralph Garbellano, at the helm. At the time, it was located on the corners of Albany Street, Watt Street, and Jackson Avenue in Schenectady, New York.

Bob started early in the automotive business, helping his father part-time after school. He paid attention and learned the business well, going full-time when he graduated. By the mid 1980s, Ralph had retired, and Bob had completely taken over G & M Affiliates.

June 1994 was a big month for Bob. He had outgrown his present facility, and decided to take on a partner. He moved to their present location, 1505 State Street, formed a partnership with Michael Rogan, and added auto sales to his already successful business.

G & M HAS NEW HOME

Bob Garbellano and Michael Rogan proudly announce the relocation of G & M Service to 1505 State Street, formerly of 1735 Union St. Their new name will be **G & M Auto Tech, Inc.**

Forty years ago, G & M Service was founded by Ralph Garbellano and has a reputation of service excellence and fairness throughout the Schenectady area.

Bob Garbellano, who has been partners with his father for the past twenty years, has been able to carry on the family tradition and keep the business up to speed with today's ever changing technically advanced cars.

Michael Rogan, co-owner, has been a General Motors and ASE Master Technician for the past nine consecutive years, and specialized in Cadillac and other GM repair. They both are looking forward to providing quality service to customers new and old.

Michael brought his expertise to G & M Auto Tech as an ASE Certified Master Technician, and an AC Delco Master Technician. Bob is also ASE Certified, and regularly attends continuing education classes with AC Delco Management and A.S.I.A.

Bob's son, Bryan, had worked with his father at G & M since he was thirteen years old, as Bob did with his father, but Bryan decided to take a different path. He joined the Coast Guard in May of 1999 and spent most of his four years in Rochester on Lake Ontario. Today, he is a Marine interdiction agent for the U.S. Customs and Border Patrol, as well as a special agent with U.S. Coast Guard Investigative Services in the Reserves. Bryan is presently working in Michigan.

Bob attributes their success to their commitment to service and quality work in a very clean facility. They offer the latest in diagnostic equipment and their technicians keep up with the latest training courses available. According to Bob, his is a "well-oiled" business.

For additional information on G & M Auto Tech, stop by the shop or please visit www.gmautotech.com on the Internet.

G & M
AUTO TECH

GLEN SANDERS MANSION

Whether planning a luxurious weekend getaway or the wedding of your dreams, Glen Sanders Mansion is the perfect choice. The Mansion is located in Scotia, New York, on the banks of the Mohawk River, just minutes from downtown Schenectady and major attractions of the Capital Region. It offers a plethora of sights and sounds and tastes to satisfy the most discriminating traveler or bride-to-be.

One major draw of the Glen Sanders Mansion is its rich history. The Mansion is actually named for two separate families who played integral parts in the local history. Alexander Lindsey Glen, an immigrant from Scotland, was the first settler on the north side of the Mohawk River in 1658. As an agent for the Dutch West India Company, Glen built the original stone house as a trading post for the well traversed Mohawk Valley by trappers from the north. Due to flooding, Glen salvaged whatever materials he could and constructed a new one room dwelling another 100 feet from the river. This is the kitchen of the present day facility. Additions were made along the way expanding the house to a hall and three rooms. You can still see the original Dutch gambrel roof intact today.

In 1713, Glen's son added the east wing where the dining room and

Maquas Lounge is housed today. The Glen family's home was graced by many notable historic characters including General George Washington and Louis Philippe of France, while in exile.

Glen's great-granddaughter, Deborah Glen, married John Sanders of Albany, in 1739, and became the sole owners of the Glen Estate in 1765, thus making it known as the Glen Sanders Mansion. The Mansion was handed down through the generations of the Glen family until 1961.

In the seventeenth century wing of the house, lies the West Cellar, which today serves as the restaurant's wine cellar and the backdrop of a true story where a Jesuit priest "escaped through a keyhole."

Around 1685 the Mohawk Indians captured a Jesuit priest and had encamped near Glen's house. The Indians asked Glen to hold their

prisoner until the following morning at which time they would torture and kill him. Glen appeared to agree to the plan, but had one of his own. Glen warned the Indians that priests had magical powers and could escape through keyholes. Early the next morning, Glen clandestinely hid the priest in a large salt keg headed for Albany. This act of bravery in the face of the ruthless Mohawks afforded the present generation the opportunity to enjoy this historic artifact, for in saving the priest, Glen spared his home and family from the Schenectady Massacre of 1690.

A legend of the West Cellar also circulates today of an Underground Railroad tunnel from this cellar to the public library across the street. While this has not been substantiated, the driveway of the Mansion does sink every spring along that path.

The Great Room, where the main dining room is located, dates back to 1713. It boasts of the original small paned windows and an original interior Dutch door. The dining table located adjacent to this door is a popular request among guests.

Other dining areas include the Deborah Glen Room, dating back to the late seventeenth century, featuring the original woodwork, mantel, and door paneling hosting parties up to sixteen guests, along with the Alexander Glen Room, and the Stockade Room with original hand carved beams and traditional colonial style accommodating up to thirty guests for dinner or private meetings.

Larger rooms are available for meetings and wedding receptions including the Mohawk Room, the most private setting the Mansion has to offer with seating up to seventy. The Grand Salon, pristinely decorated with rich wood and crystal chandeliers, is ideal for more

intimate weddings, anniversary parties and private business meetings.

One of the area's most favored locations for wedding receptions, fundraisers, and business meetings is the Mansion's Riverfront Ballroom. Fashioned after the elegance and grandeur of the Mansion, its rich décor and over 300 seat capacity is the perfect backdrop for the most elegant wedding reception or impressive business meeting. An additional area adjacent to the Ballroom is the covered patio with an exquisite view of the Mansion's gardens. Many an outside wedding has been performed in the gardens with its charming gazebo on the banks of the Mohawk River.

The Main Lobby was created with amazing attention to detail, taking great care to alter the original structure as little as possible. It serves as a spacious entrance for the Mansion's restaurant, meeting rooms, and the Inn, added in 1995. The Inn was meticulously designed to blend with the original facade of the Mansion creating an almost seamless continuance of the seventeenth century structure.

The Inn includes twenty delightful, well-appointed overnight rooms and two luxurious suites, all of which boast a perfect blending of the preservation of the past with the convenience of modern amenities. Both the Glen Suite and Sanders Suite will take your breath away with their romantic fireplace to curl up in front of after soaking in the inviting Jacuzzi made for two.

After a restful night in the plush king-size poster bed, take a trip to the lobby where you will be greeted with the divine scent of freshly-made waffles and fresh fruit as part of the Mansion's enticing breakfast bar open to its guests. A sitting area with comfy couches and

stone fireplace complete the warm ambiance of the gracious hospitality of a time gone by.

The Glen Sanders Mansion is a charming retreat for anyone who appreciates breathtaking scenery and luxurious surroundings, but the crowning touch of the Mansion is the warmth and hospitality you feel from the dedicated,

obliging staff. According to owner Angelo Mazzone, "We strive to exceed our guests' expectations, accommodate their desires, and make each event, meal, and stay in our Inn as memorable as possible."

For more information, including rates and reservations, visit www.glensandersmansion.com.

NORTHEASTERN
FINE JEWELRY

Whether you are searching for the perfect gift or the most exquisite bridal set, you need look no further than Northeastern Fine Jewelry. It is unequivocally the largest and finest jeweler in the Capital District with four locations to serve its clients: 1607 Union Street, Schenectady; 1575 Western Avenue, Albany; 4620 Main Street, Manchester Center, Vermont, and the newest additionin downtown Schenectady at 432 State Street adjacent to Proctor's Theater. Starting in 1980 with Northeastern Coin Gallery, Raymond A. Bleser's philosophy, "give the customer unbeatable service and quality merchandise at the best value" proved to be his greatest business strategy.

Within five years of starting his initial storefront, Ray purchased and renovated the facility at 1607 Union Street in Schenectady thus giving birth to Northeastern Fine Jewelry.

Business surpassed Ray's expectations during the next two decades and by 2004 he had opened two additional locations in Albany, New York, and Manchester Center, Vermont.

To visit Northeastern Fine Jewelry's locations is a treat in itself. While at the Albany location, you can relax with a beverage and a cookie while catching up on the latest news on the many big screen televisions. If you have little ones along, Northeastern offers a diversion with their play area, which includes video games and cartoons.

Manchester Center, Vermont, is a stunning showroom with its marble counter tops, chandeliers, and cozy fireplace to enjoy while perusing the newest lines of world-class jewelry.

Northeastern Fine Jewelry is a member of the Leading Jewelers of the World and an exclusive member of the Continental Buying Group. It is proud of its ongoing compliance with LJW's Diamond Best-Practice Principles. It specializes in white and fancy-yellow diamonds, bridal jewelry, gold, and platinum. It is equipped to handle jewelry and watch repairs, along with custom design and fabrication service.

Northeastern Fine Jewelry has a knowledgeable staff including two master jewelers, four graduate gemologists, five bench jewelers, and three National Association of Jewelry Appraiser (NAJA) members dedicated to exceeding their clients' satisfaction.

For more information, please visit Northeastern Fine Jewelry at www.nefj.com.

Above: Northeastern Fine Jewelry located at 1607 Union Street in Schenectady, New York.

Below: Northeastern Fine Jewelry located at 1575 Western Avenue in Albany, New York.

STOCKADE INN

Located in the charming historic Stockade District, The Stockade Inn is a beautifully restored structure purchased in 2003 by the McDonald family. Jeff McDonald, his father, Jack, and his mother, JoAnn, felt a great responsibility to such an historic landmark, painstakingly updating the facility to modern standards while maintaining its historic authenticity. The outcome has been a perfect blending of high-end luxury with an old-world flavor, the best of both worlds.

Both Jeff and Jack are successful engineers in their own right and are actively involved in their community. Jack owns an engineering firm, John M. McDonald Engineering P.C., while also serving as a board member of the Downtown Schenectady Improvement Corporation. Jeff, at the beginning of 2008, was elected for a four-year term as county legislator, earning him the title of one of the youngest elected officials at the age of twenty-eight. He was quoted in *The Daily Gazette*, "I have a vested interest in the county and I can't wait to

be part of the decision-making process." Jeff also serves as a member of the City of Schenectady Industrial Development Agency, and was the recipient of the *Business Review*'s "40 under 40" Award.

The McDonalds have a reputation for high caliber service and impeccable culinary delights as seen in their well known eating establishment, "Pinhead Susan's," a popular eatery and pub in the District. Being familiar with the restaurant environment, the McDonald's already possessed the knowledge and experience to transform the property at the corner of Union and Church Streets into a fine dining establishment along with the historic inn it has become today. But this was not always so for this little corner of the world.

In the seventeenth century a Dutch immigrant, Arendt Van Curler, learning early the language of the Mohawk Indians and cultivating a friendship with them, purchased from the Mohawks a tract of land called "the Great Flat." The tract was subdivided into lots with Van Curler's site at the corner where the Stockade Inn is located today. Since housing the Van Curler family in the late seventeenth century, the tract was used for the Sheriff of Schenectady and a drinking establishment before being burned by the French and Indians in 1690. It served as a

private residence through the eighteenth century and became the location of the Mohawk Bank in the early 1800s complete with a block vault in the basement. Most of the building we see today was constructed in 1818 with numerous additions through the years bringing it to its current size of ten thousand square feet.

During the middle 1800s the site became a private residence and in 1872, the building was purchased by the Union School, an early representation of the current public school system. The lengthiest ownership of the site was

Above: President's Grille Ballroom

Below: Abraham Yates Room.

Above: Billard room.

Below: Stockade Inn Bar.

delightful fine dining establishment and a well-appointed charming retreat from the hustle and bustle of the modern world just outside the Inn's preserved historic walls.

The Stockade Inn offers a variety of appointments catering to a range of uses from business meetings to weddings and receptions. Their meeting rooms include the beautifully decorated Van Curler Room with seating for forty to seventy, which is ideal for private parties, rehearsal dinners, or showers. The elegant President's/Grille Ballroom, recently renovated, is perfect for weddings with guest seating up to 140, and the Trustees Room, the most intimate meeting place for 10 to 20, caters to corporate business meetings with high-speed Internet access and audio visual amenities.

If you want to feel as if you have stepped back in time, you may want to reserve the Billiards Room for your private function, a warmly authentic room complete with antique billiard tables, a beautiful oak-finished open beam ceiling, and polished original wood flooring. It accommodates up to twenty-five for private sit down functions and up to forty for cocktails.

The Stockade Inn bar, The Oak Room, now occupies the space once used as the Mohawk Club business office and includes an imported antique copper topped bar and oak-finished open beam ceiling. To satisfy your appetite, they offer the Lounge with lighter fare and accompanying libations, or for a more intimate dinner for two or a family affair, you may prefer the elegant main dining room offering a wide variety of mouth-watering appetizers, entrees, and homemade desserts.

For your overnight stay, you may have a difficult time choosing between The Stockade Inn's charming suites and rooms. There are eighteen rooms available including a romantic bridal suite, the Abraham Yates Room, the Widow Kendall Room, and the Adam Vrooman Room, all blending antique furnishings with the best of modern amenities, a combination of past and present sure to delight even seasoned travelers.

With forty employees, you are sure to experience the gracious hospitality of days gone by. For a glimpse of Stockade Inn's facilities, directions or general information, please visit www.stockadeinn.com.

by far the Mohawk Club, "a private men's social club" who purchased the building in 1904. Private men's clubs were in vogue around the turn of the century and this one was no exception with a history dating back to 1885. The Mohawk Club, known as an exclusive location for dining, entertainment, and business meetings for men only, boasted a membership of over 600 during their most successful era. The Club still meets today at The Stockade Inn in one of their beautifully restored meeting rooms.

Since transfer of ownership from The Mohawk Club to the McDonald family in 2003, major renovations have been completed. The renovations transformed the Inn into a

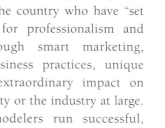

The magazine selects fifty companies from around the country who have "set the standard for professionalism and integrity through smart marketing, exemplary business practices, unique design, and extraordinary impact on their community or the industry at large. "Big 50" remodelers run successful, growing companies that have taken the lead in raising the industry standards."

Bellamy Construction is a full-service building and remodeling company, including additions and decks, basement remodeling, excavation, insurance restoration, and building its client's custom designed home. Its mission statement says it all: "Tell us your dream. We at Bellamy Construction will listen, and together we will make that dream a reality for you and your family. We're a family business, and we proudly bring to your project our core values of excellence, integrity, and safety, plus our solid reputation in the community. Nothing comes second with Bellamy Construction. From start to finish, every phase of your project will reflect the Bellamy philosophy: putting our pride in your home and creating superior results—guaranteed."

Bellamy Construction is located at 6684 Amsterdam Road in Scotia and on the Internet at www.bellamys.com.

Starting their remodeling company in 1975, Bruce and Sharon Bellamy incorporated in 1994 under the name Bellamy & Sons Construction, Inc. Since that time, the company has grown to include Bruce and Sharon's sons, Greg and Brian, and their wives, Katie and Tanya. The company serves Scotia, Schenectady, Saratoga, Albany, and the Capital District areas. Today, it is growing and adapting to an ever-changing market which includes the name change to Bellamy Construction.

Bellamy Construction has always been proud to support the wonderful community projects in and around Schenectady County, such as the Joan Nicole Prince Hospice House, Habitat for Humanity, the Flint House, Community Gardens, and the Scotia Glenville School District, including a yearly scholarship for a graduating senior entering a college construction program. Along with these local organizations, the company also supports Juvenile Diabetes Research Foundation, and many other volunteer building and excavation projects.

In 2003, Bellamy & Sons, Inc. received the prestigious induction into the "Big 50" by *Remodeling* magazine.

SCHENECTADY COUNTY COMMUNITY COLLEGE

Above: The Hotel Van Curler was once a landmark on Washington Avenue in Schenectady. The former hotel was converted into the main classroom building, now Elston Hall, and SCCC began offering classes in the building in September 1969.

Below: SCCC graduates are prepared to transfer to four-year institutions or to enter the workforce through the College's transfer and career degree programs, as well as certificate programs.

The elegant Van Curler Hotel opened in 1925 on Washington Avenue in Schenectady. The grand hotel enticed guests by advertising "Dining during the summer on Mohawk Terrace overlooking the river and the great Western Gateway Bridge." After decades of serving as a landmark in Schenectady, the hotel closed its doors to guests on February 2, 1968.

At the same time that the hotel was entering its final phase, the Board of Supervisors of Schenectady County, on April 13, 1965, appointed a group of forty-nine citizens to a special Community College Study Committee to assess the desirability for and feasibility of a community college in Schenectady. In 1966 the Committee reported that a community college would be an asset to Schenectady. The Board of Supervisors of Schenectady County passed a resolution accepting and approving a positive report by the Committee on December 30, 1966, later designating the Hotel Van Curler as the College's location.

In September 1969, SCCC opened its doors to the first entering class, offering eight transfer and career degree programs with 39 full-time faculty and 654 full-time and 632 part-time students. The building was renamed Elston Hall, in honor of Charles W. Elston, a member of the original Board of Trustees who served as Chair of the Board for eight years. This main building now houses a Student Center with a cafeteria; a student lounge; the College Bookstore; the Casola Dining Room, a gourmet restaurant open to the public which serves as a teaching tool for students in the Culinary Arts Department; biology, geology, and culinary arts laboratories; classrooms; meeting rooms; and offices; and an enclosed pedestrian bridge connecting Elston Hall with the Center for Science and Technology.

The campus now includes four additional buildings: the Begley Building, completed in 1978, which houses the Begley Library; an Instructional Technology Center; a video-conferencing studio; a Music Wing for nationally accredited music programs; and the Carl B. Taylor Community Auditorium; the

Center for Science and Technology, acquired in 1987, with the College's physics and chemistry labs, as well as specialized lab facilities for electrical technology, computer science and nanoscale materials technology; the Gateway Building, opened in March 2000, which contains Early Childhood classes and labs, the Gateway Montessori Preschool and a child care center; and the Stockade Building, which opened in Fall 2001 and has electronic and traditional classrooms, two lecture halls, the Continuing Education Division, Workforce Development programs and conference rooms. Also, an enclosed walkway links Elston Hall and the Begley Building with the Stockade Building.

A $6.3-million Culinary Arts Addition to Elston Hall was completed in August 2007 and features two new laboratories, a dedicated kitchen for the Casola Dining Room, a seminar room and a gourmet dining room. The College's new Campus Master Plan includes an addition to the Music Wing in the Begley Building, acquisition of property across Washington Avenue, a walkway over Washington Avenue and a new Business Center.

The College has as its mission to "provide quality, comprehensive higher education to meet the career, transfer, training, cultural and lifelong learning needs of the individual, the community and the workforce" and it is committed to making education accessible and affordable to a population with diverse backgrounds, needs, and aspirations. SCCC is able to fulfill this mission through flexible course schedules, small class sizes, and superb faculty. In fact, over forty-five faculty and staff members have been recognized with SUNY Chancellor's Awards for Excellence. In addition to teaching, SCCC faculty are authors, chefs, scientists, mathematicians, lawyers, and musicians.

Since its inception in 1969, over 13,600 students have graduated from SCCC and thousands more have taken courses at the College with programs leading to the degrees of Associate in Arts, Associate in Science, Associate in Applied Science, Associate in Occupational Studies, and one-year certificates. The College currently enrolls nearly five thousand students. Programs include: Accounting, Aviation Science, Business Administration, Chemical Dependency Counseling, Computer Science, Criminal Justice, Culinary Arts, Drama, Early Childhood, Electrical Technology, Emergency Management, Fire Protection Technology, Health Studies, Hotel and Restaurant Management, Human Services, Liberal Arts: Humanities/Social Sciences, Mathematics/Science, Music, Nanoscale Materials Technology, Paralegal, Science, Teacher Education Transfer, Teaching Assistant, and

❖

Above: Visitors from the Capital Region and beyond enjoy savory meals in the College's popular Casola Dining Room, a gourmet restaurant open to the public. The dining room provides an opportunity for students to gain experience in a wide range of dining room and banquet service activities.

Below: Students gather in the College's Quad, a scenic area of campus, to study, relax, or socialize. The campus includes five buildings: Elston Hall, the Center for Science and Technology, Stockade Building, Begley Building and the Gateway Building.

Tourism and Hospitality Management. The College also offers non-credit courses for local business and industry, as well as professional and personal development courses.

SCCC is one of thirty community colleges in the SUNY (State University of New York) system which entitles students with A.A. or A.S. degrees guaranteed admission to a SUNY senior college. Through transfer agreements with over thirty institutions, students may transfer to other colleges with junior status.

SCCC is accredited by the Middle States Association of Colleges and Schools, Commission on Higher Education. The College is also an accredited institutional member of the National Association of Schools of Music. The Paralegal program is approved by the American Bar Association; Business programs are accredited by the Association of Collegiate Business Schools and Programs; the Culinary Arts A.O.S. degree program is approved by the American Culinary Federation Foundation Accrediting Commission; and the Culinary Arts Baking Concentration is approved by the Retailer's Bakery Association.

The College continues to offer the latest in cutting-edge technology through electronic classrooms, a videoconferencing center, wireless access, online courses, and state-of-the-art laboratories including physics, electronics and vacuum science labs.

Also, through a successful partnership between SCCC and SUNY, Delhi students take all courses on the SCCC campus in two Delhi programs: Hospitality Management B.B.A degree and Management of Technology B.B.A. degree.

Throughout its history, SCCC has transformed the lives of thousands of students, providing them with a bridge to career training and higher education that is affordable and accessible, helping them to achieve their goals.

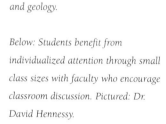

Above: Students gain hands-on learning experience through the College's labs, including those for chemistry, physics, biology, and geology.

Below: Students benefit from individualized attention through small class sizes with faculty who encourage classroom discussion. Pictured: Dr. David Hennessy.

VINCY'S PRINTING

Vincy's Printing is well known in the Rotterdam and surrounding areas for high quality, professional printing and design. A third generation company, Vincy's has a proven track record of producing quality work while offering outstanding customer service.

Vincy's Printing had its humble beginning during the late 1960s in the home of Anthony Vinciguerra at the corner of Altamont and Crane Streets in Rotterdam. Tony Denning, the owner of Vincy's Printing today, recalls his fascination of the printing business in his grandfather's home even as a small boy. His interest grew after his mother, Evelyn Vinciguerra Lessner, purchased the business from her father, Anthony, in 1978. Under Evelyn's direction, Vincy's Printing flourished.

Tony started with the company in 1986 as a press operator. With no formal training, he learned the business as a self-taught, hands-on apprentice. He absorbed as much as possible about the printing business during these years, and in 1998, purchased the company from his mother.

Since Tony acquired Vincy's Printing, it has grown to a staff of ten printing professionals and offers complete graphic design in both Mac and PC platforms. As a full-service commercial printer, Vincy's does more than just design, copy, and print; it enable its customers to communicate. Effective communication is vital to inform, impress, and inspire others. With Vincy's state-of-the-art technology, it does just that with the highest quality standards in the area, offering an outstanding degree of excellence in multicolor production along with the best customer service in the business.

Vincy's Printing has been in operation for almost forty years surviving an ever changing economic environment. Tony attributes the company's success to the company's dedication to customer satisfaction. It strives to delight every customer every time.

Be sure to visit the company's new location at 1832 Curry Road, Rotterdam, New York. For more information, please call (518) 355-4363 or visit www.vincysprinting.com.

Above: Vincy's Printing's original Location opened by Anthony Vinciguerra.

Below: The company's new location at 1832 Curry Road, Rotterdam, New York.

KINGSWAY COMMUNITY

Kingsway Community, the only retirement community in the region to offer a continuum of care on one convenient campus, was founded in 1975. The facility resulted from the vision of a local dentist, Dr. J. Peter McPartlon, who wanted to have a place in Schenectady dedicated to seniors where they could feel welcome and well cared for.

Dr. McPartlon and a partner, R. Michael Sessa, constructed Kingsway Community, which was Schenectady County's first combination proprietary nursing home and health related facility. Soon after opening, Dr. McPartlon bought out Sessa to become the sole owner.

Dr. McPartlon's daughter, Anne Marie, joined Kingsway in 1983 and became administrator of Kingsway Arms in 1991. She retired in 2002. Son Michael began working at Kingsway in 1993 and is now vice president/chief operating officer of Kingsway Community, and oversees the day-to-day business operations. The facility employs approximately 450 individuals.

Top: Kingsway Village Apartments.

Middle: Parkland Garden Apartments.

Bottom: Kingsway Court Apartments.

Kingsway Community opened in 1975 with Kingsway Arms Nursing Center. Kingsway Court Apartments, a twelve-unit apartment building was added four years later. In 1985, Parkland Garden Apartments was added to the community, offering sixty-five units ranging from studio apartments to one-and-two-bedroom apartments. Kingsway Manor Assisted Living Residence, a 120-bed licensed adult home, was built in 1991. Kingsway Kids Center, an on-site child daycare center, was also added to the community in 1991.

Kingsway Home Care Services, Inc. opened in 1997, providing licensed home care service to a five-county area within the Capital District. This was followed by KingsDay Adult Social Day Service in 1997 and Kingsway Respite Service in 2001.

Growth continued in 2001 with the opening of Kingsway Village Apartments. This 104-unit apartment building offers one-and-two bedroom apartments, as well as some one-bedroom with den apartments.

A twenty bed Memory Care Center, currently under construction, is scheduled to open in 2010. This new wing of the Skilled Nursing Center will join the skilled nursing facility to the assisted living residence.

Today, Kingsway Community is a senior residential community offering a complete continuum of care that includes senior independent living apartments, adult day service, respite, home care, assisted living, rehabilitation, skilled nursing, child daycare and car service.

Kingsway Kids Center is an integral part of the campus, allowing for stimulating intergenerational programs between the children and residents. The Center also helps in the recruitment of staff members who need quality daycare for their children. The proximity of the Kids Center allows for parent visits during lunch or break time.

Kingsway Community's twenty-five acre campus is located at 323 Kings Road in Schenectady. Approximately 460 residents live on campus within various buildings, and about sixty children attend daycare Monday through Friday.

Every year for the past fifteen years, Kingsway Community has sponsored and coordinated a golf tournament with all proceeds going to the Make-A-Wish foundation of Northeast New York. Over the years, more than $200,000 has been raised to benefit local children who have a life-threatening medical condition. On average, the event attracts 90 to 100 golfers and more than 40 sponsors. The event features a child who has had a wish granted. The wish recipients relate their stories and are a source of inspiration to tournament participants.

For more information about Kingsway Community, visit www.kingswaycommunity.com.

Kingsway Community is the only retirement community in the region to offer a continuum of care on one convenient campus.

KNOLLS ATOMIC POWER LABORATORY

Knolls Atomic Power Laboratory (KAPL) provides nuclear propulsion systems for U.S. Navy ships by designing the world's most technologically advanced, safe, and reliable reactor plants and systems, supporting the operating fleet of nuclear ships and training the sailors who operate them. The employees of KAPL, and the technology they work on every day, are a vital part of our nation's defense. Nuclear powered ships comprise forty-five percent of the Navy's combat fleet, including 100 percent of the submarine fleet. KAPL's work has been instrumental in sustaining the Naval Reactors Program's unparalleled record—over 139 million miles steamed on nuclear power, and over 5,900 reactor years of safe operation.

KAPL, managed under contract by Bechtel Marine Propulsion Corporation since February 2009, operates two sites in Tech Valley. In Niskayuna, the Knolls site is home to about 2,100 employees working in design and development facilities including engineering offices, laboratories, computing and test facilities, and a radioactive materials laboratory in which the technology and materials of nuclear reactors are tested and studied. Fundamental research in related sciences is also performed. In West Milton, the Kesselring site is home to about 500 employees and 1,300 U.S. Navy personnel. Here, prototype nuclear propulsion plants are operated and tested, and future Navy submarine and aircraft carrier personnel are trained.

On May 15, 1946, the Knolls Atomic Power Laboratory began with a contract between General Electric Company and the United States Government. KAPL's purpose in 1946 was to

conduct nuclear research and development, including work on a plant design that would use nuclear energy—rather than fossil fuel—for generating electricity. In 1950 the nuclear power plant project was converted to a Naval nuclear propulsion project.

KAPL was one of the first laboratories to conduct research work on obtaining usable power from nuclear reactors. By 1955, KAPL had designed a reactor that could propel a submarine for about three years of operations. A prototype of that design was built and operated at the laboratory's Kesselring site. The first shipboard application of the design was in the submarine *Seawolf* (SSN 575), which was commissioned in 1957. Since then, KAPL has designed several larger and more powerful reactors for use in nuclear powered submarines and surface ships.

Reactor plants designed by KAPL currently power the *Los Angeles Class* attack submarines, *Ohio Class* ballistic and guided missile submarines, *Nimitz Class* nuclear aircraft carriers, and the world's most technologically advanced new attack submarines, the *Virginia Class.*

KAPL also provides technical support to the nuclear fleet, supporting currently commissioned ships that use KAPL designed reactor plants and cores, as well as new construction and decommissioning activities. It also manages and assists in the operation of land-based Naval nuclear propulsion plants that are platforms for training Naval personnel and testing of new designs and technologies. Over 60,000 sailors have been trained at KAPL land-based nuclear propulsion plants. We continue to train 1,200 sailors each year.

At KAPL, one of our core values is to "do what's right," which means we are committed to being a valued partner in the community, focused on enhancing the quality of life in the communities where we live and work. In 2007, KAPL's volunteer organization, the NOVA Society, conducted over sixty community programs, and employees personally volunteered over 20,000 hours of their time. KAPL employees also donated $289,000 to United Way of the Greater Capital Region, which was matched with a $55,000 corporate donation.

For over sixty years, KAPL has been dedicated to the Naval Nuclear Propulsion Program and Schenectady County, providing leadership in one of the most remarkable engineering programs in the world. Yet it is the dedication of all the employees that has made KAPL what it is today—a world-class national resource.

For more information about KAPL, visit www.knollslab.com.

LANGE'S PHARMACY

For the Lange family, pharmacology has been a way of life since the early twentieth century. Otto Lange was the first in the family to attend Albany College of Pharmacy. The college was only a two-year school at the time Otto graduated in 1919, but is now a six year program. He was a young graduate, only nineteen years of age. Too young to obtain a license as a pharmacist, he stayed at the college and taught school with one of his classmates, Francis O'Brien. Francis stayed at Albany College of Pharmacy and eventually became the Dean, but Otto pursued his dream of one day having his own store, which is now run by his grandchildren, Dan and David Lange.

Otto went to work at Walker Pharmacy on State Street in Schenectady in the early 1920s. He worked diligently and learned all he could about operating a pharmacy until 1936, when he, and one of his co-workers, Abe Rapp, left to open a store together. The Lange & Rapp Pharmacy sat at the corner of State Street and Nott Terrace in Schenectady. At this time, General Electric was also located in Schenectady with a workforce numbering into the tens of thousands. Lange & Rapp supplied a patented medicine called GE liniment (a rub for sore muscles) to the workers at the GE plant. Even though people still ask for it today, it is no longer offered due to the unavailability of some ingredients.

Otto and his partner branched out into a satellite pharmacy purchased in Niskayuna in 1960. They kept the original name, Mahoney's, and operated it as such until 1963. Lange's Pharmacy still has the same phone number today dating back to the 1950s from Mahoney's Pharmacy, FR4-3324 or 374-3324.

Fritz Lange, Dan and David's father, followed in his father's footsteps attending Albany College of Pharmacy, and graduating in 1958. Fritz

purchased the business at Mahoney's, becoming the sole owner in 1963. He changed the name to Lange's Pharmacy in 1964, thus starting the original pharmacy still in operation today.

The pharmacy sold everything from books to cosmetics and toiletries. Every year during the Christmas season, "Santa" (Fritz Lange) visited the store so the local children could have their picture taken on Santa's knee.

In 1975, Lange's Pharmacy moved from its location at 2207 Nott Street just two doors down to its present location at 2205 Nott Street in Niskayuna. It was during this time the pharmacy discontinued its sale of various sundries with a few exceptions, concentrating its energies on providing only prescription medicine.

Lange's was the first pharmacy in the county to stop selling tobacco items in the 1980s due to the urging of Dan and David's uncle, Dr. Richard Lange of Ellis Hospital. He felt it was not right for a healthcare facility to sell something that was considered to be so unhealthy.

Otto's brother, Gilbert Lange, also opened a Lange's Pharmacy in Lake George, which was in business for many years. Dan Lange, after spending six years in the Navy right out of high school, was unsure of the direction he should take. He was encouraged by his mother to join his younger brother, David, and older sister, Betsy, at Albany College of Pharmacy. He graduated from the college in 1992. David and Betsy graduated in 1989. Both David and Dan married graduates of ACP. Dan's wife, Angel,

graduated in 1989, while David's wife, Jean, graduated in 1990.

In the 1960s, there were over fifty independent pharmacies in Schenectady County and only two chains. Today, there are only two independent pharmacies left. Lange's Pharmacy has survived the onslaught of the mega stores with a loyal following that still appreciate the one on one customer service only Lange's can offer. Just like their grandfather, Otto, did over seventy years ago, Dan, David, and Angel, still offer compounding services, local delivery to shut-ins, in-store accounts, and personal family service.

Be sure to visit Lange's Pharmacy at 2205 Nott Street in Niskayuna, or for more information, call (518) 374-3324.

❖

Above: Lange & Rapp at corner of State Street and Nott Terrace, c. the 1940s.

Below: Abe Rapp (far right) and Otto Lange (far right) at Walker's Pharmacy, c. the 1930s.

SILAR LABORATORIES

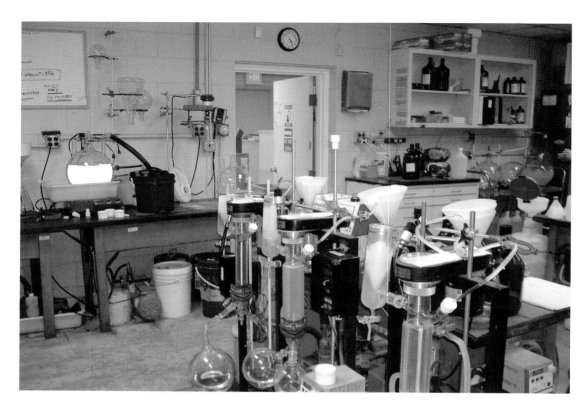

Above: Testing Laboratory.

Below: Silane Production Laboratory.

Silar Laboratories was founded in Scotia, New York, in 1972, by Art Coleman and Terry Selin. Both founders earned Ph.D.s in chemistry, and have over thirty years experience in developing and producing silicon-based products. The name of the company was to have been the combination of the two doctors' names, "Sel" from Terry Selin, and "ar" from Art Coleman. Due to a printing error, "Silar" not "Selar" was formed. The doctors, realizing the obvious correlation between the erroneous name and the silane compounds the company produced, made the decision to stay with the error.

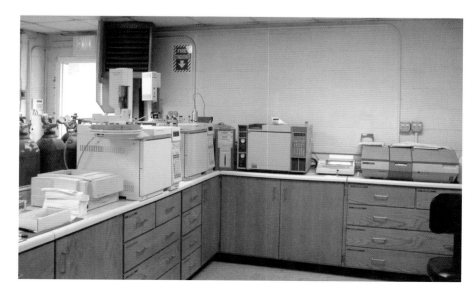

The name may have been in error, but forming Silar Laboratories definitely was not. It has more than doubled in size in the Scotia, New York area alone. The Scotia production facilities sit on three acres and have the ability to handle gram to multi-kilo orders as well as developing new projects. Bob Rusinko and Steve Tetrick, both with Ph.D. degrees in chemistry, run the local Silar Laboratories today.

In 1991, Silar Laboratories was purchased by Wright Chemical Corporation (not to be confused with the first family in flight), a North Carolina family owned company for four generations, whose predecessor in the chemical business was founded in 1883. Wright Chemical Corporation began in 1959 as a liquid alum plant. Under their ownership, Silar Laboratories' capabilities were expanded with a larger sized production facility located in Acme, North Carolina. Corporate headquarters is located a short distance away in Wilmington, North Carolina, in the oldest structure still standing in the area, built in 1740. John Shibley, Ph.D., who heads up all Silar Laboratories operations, has his office in the Wilmington corporate office.

In 2004, Oak-Bark Corporation was formed as a result of a management buy-out of most assets owned by Wright Chemical Corporation. OBC's current businesses include Silar

Laboratories Division, Pharmaceutical Products Plant, and Special and Dry Products, each with their own areas of expertise. Oak-Bark Corporation Chairman Bill Oakley, has been with WCC and OBC since 1978.

Since its inception, Silar Laboratories has been dedicated to producing the highest quality silicon-based products, organosilanes, for pharmaceutical, electronics, industrial, and specialty chemical use, and continues its research to find leading-edge chemical compounds. Silar has special expertise in the manufacture of compounds used in the production of hard and soft contact lenses.

At the present time, Silar produces approximately 300 distinct silane compounds per year with the capability of producing up to 1000, including, but not limited to alkoxysilanes, blocking agents, silazanes, silicone monomers, silane coupling reagents, and specialty silicone polymers. They perform custom and toll conversions on a proprietary basis with production areas well equipped to handle various types of chemicals on a regular basis. Their customers have audited the facilities on many occasions for compliance with their quality, environmental and safety criteria.

Silar Laboratories, as part of its parent company, Oak-Bark Corporation, consistently strives in its Research and Development department to find the newest chemical compounds to transform pharmaceutical and computer-technology based companies in their future endeavors.

One distinct characteristic of Silar Laboratories, as well as all of Oak-Bark subsidiaries, is its insight into the importance of taking care of its own. Oak-Bark's commitment to the welfare of their employees is second to none. Oak-Bark is a family friendly company that encourages employee loyalty by sharing corporate profits with its staff. The ongoing research into new chemicals helps insure job security well into the future.

For further information, general inquiries, or contact information, visit the Silar Laboratories, Inc., website at www.oak-bark.com.

Above: Front Row: (Left to Right) Mike, Bob, and Erik. Back Row: Mark, Steve, and Greg.

Below: GC Analysis.

BAPTIST HEALTH NURSING AND REHABILITATION CENTER

Baptist Health Nursing and Rehabilitation Center has touched the lives of many, from residents to the family members who love them. The dedicated, caring staff brings to life their motto, "People Caring for People." Baptist Health Nursing and Rehabilitation Center provides twenty-four hour long-term, skilled nursing care, as well as long and short term rehabilitative services. The philosophy for Baptist Health is to become an extension of home, offering superior care in a loving environment, delicious and appetizing food prepared on the premises, companionship along with fellowship, and an engaging variety of activities to provide and sustain the highest quality of life for our residents. A distinct feature at Baptist Health is the extremely caring staff that treats the residents who come to live there as they would their own family.

In 2007, Baptist Health Nursing and Rehabilitation Center celebrated their thirtieth anniversary. Their facility in Scotia, New York

was selected to receive the 2007 Public Trust Award from the American Association of Homes and Services for the Aging. They were recognized for setting a higher standard in providing services and information to seniors

❖

Above: A Baptist Health Nursing and Rehabilitation Center resident, Anastasia Barr, enjoying her first ever pedicure while dressed in her new outfit that was part of her "Dreams Can Come True" Spa Day.

Below: Kieran, one of Baptist Health Nursing and Rehabilitation Center's on-premise therapy dogs, along with Marketing Director Ruth Tietz, bringing a smile to a resident's face on "National Make Someone Smile Day."

with their "Six on Seniors" television news segment that airs on Mondays during the Noon Newscast on WRGB. An exciting, new program was just recently introduced which is similar to "Make-A-Wish." Nominated residents are given an experience they have only dreamed of through "Dreams Can Come True." "We had one resident in her 90s who used to love doing girly things, so we brought her out for a day at the spa," said Marketing, Public Relations and Development Director, Ruth Tietz. "She had a manicure and her first-ever pedicure, had her hair styled, and picked out a new outfit. It was so great to see her enjoyment." There have also been trips to Proctor's Theater and visits to local restaurants.

The Baptist Retirement Center, as it was originally known in the community, was opened on November 9, 1977, by the area American Baptist clergy and laymen. The initial facility accommodated 180 seniors with varying medical needs. By 1994 an additional eighty-two beds were added bringing the total capacity to 262 people. The new wing also includes enlarged physical therapy and occupational therapy departments where residents can participate in a sub-acute rehabilitative program that is customized based upon their specific issues and abilities.

In 1997 a restructuring of the organization took place creating Baptist Health System, the parent organization for Baptist Health Nursing and Rehabilitation Center, Baptist Health System Foundation, Family Medical Care, and The Nurse Connection Staffing, Inc.

Although the Center started as a Baptist facility, residents are not required to have an affiliation with the Baptist denomination. "We're completely non-denominational, and have residents from all faiths and spiritual beliefs," said Tietz. "We do provide venues here for people to worship from many religions; we have a full-time chaplain and relationships with many local churches and spiritual organizations."

Baptist Health Nursing and Rehabilitation Center understands the correlation between improved physical and mental health and the level of participation of the residents in every day activities. They offer a wide variety of activity choices from field trips, themed parties, to discussion groups on current events as well as

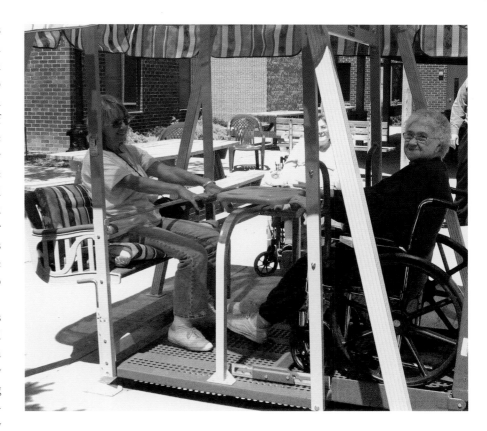

history, exercise groups, gardening, on-site therapy dogs, and much more.

Undoubtedly, Baptist Health Center's most valued asset through the years has been their staff, now numbering approximately 360 people, who have added the indispensable "human touch" to the equation. "It takes a very special and caring person to do this, and many staff members have stayed with us since day one," said President and CEO Timothy Bartos. "I can't think of any other work that's more rewarding and satisfying. At the end of the day, we know we've touched peoples' lives."

For more information about Baptist Health Nursing and Rehabilitation Center, please visit www.bapthealth.com.

❖

Above: The courtyard at Baptist Health Nursing and Rehabilitation Center is where many of our residents and their families can be found in warmer weather enjoying the wheelchair-accessible swing that was purchased by the Baptist Health System Foundation.

Below: Baptist Health Nursing and Rehabilitation Center President and CEO Timothy Bartos shown with CBS/Channel 6 Noon News Anchor Liz Bishop with the AAHSA Public Trust Award won by Baptist as a result of the "Six on Seniors" Weekly News Segment, November 2007.

PREISMAN REALTY

The Preisman family, which has had its roots in the real estate business since the 1920s, has been an integral force in the sales and building of custom homes, and in land development in Niskayuna, New York, and surrounding neighborhoods. They have enjoyed long-term success in spite of a fluctuating economy by combining a deep commitment to the community with a quality product. President Richard Preisman and son, Vice President David Preisman attribute the continued success of Preisman Realty to the strong family business heritage. Richard's grandmother, Sarah Friedman, started the family in real estate in 1925 under the name "Friedman Realty." Richard's parents, Ruth and Benjamin Preisman, joined Friedman Realty in the late 1930s. In the 1940s, they branched out into home development and began the Preisman legacy with the formation of Preisman Realty. Benjamin, a Russian-born immigrant, acquired a law degree from Brooklyn Law School and studied architectural design at Cooper Union in New York. He was considered a trailblazer in the building industry in New York, constructing homes in the Schenectady area from the 1930s to 2000. His wife, Ruth, a graduate of Russell Sage College in 1928, ran the everyday operations as office manager and bookkeeper, and continued to be very active in the business until she retired in 1999, at the age of ninety.

Benjamin devoted more than sixty years to the building industry in and around Niskayuna. He is credited with making a significant contribution to the transformation of Niskayuna from a rustic community to a thriving suburb. In 1959, Preisman Realty was featured in *American Home* magazine as the winner of the awards for the Schenectady "Best Home for the Money" and the New York State "Best Home for the Money." "My father was very proud of this recognition," said Richard.

Benjamin served as president of the Schenectady Builders and Remodelers Association in 1960-61 and president of the New York State Builders

Association in 1967. He was honored, posthumously, in 2001, when he was elected to the New York State Builders Association Hall of Fame.

Richard joined his parents' business in 1959, after graduating from Syracuse University, and soon became a realtor. He served as president of the Schenectady Home Builders Association in 1990. He also served two terms as president of the Schenectady Board of Realtors and is now president of the Schenectady Saratoga Schoharie Association of Realtors. He strongly believes in being an active participant in the organizations that serve and shape his profession, not only to keep up to date, but also to affect changes in the industry.

Continuing the Preisman legacy are the Preismans' son, David, and daughter, Sandra, making it a third-generation business. David has always been intrigued by new home construction and development, and after

graduating from Siena College in 1991, he, too, became a realtor. After building homes in Florida, he returned to his home town of Schenectady, where he is currently a builder and realtor in the Capital Region.

Following in her grandmother's footsteps, Sandra graduated from Russell Sage College in 1987 and became a realtor shortly after. She was instrumental in implementing computer technology into the business. Currently, she is a full-time employee at GE Global Research in Niskayuna.

In 2004, Preisman Realty was proud to be the featured Builder Profile in the *Empire State Builder*, the official publication of the New York State Builders Association.

Richard's wife, Barbara, a speech-language pathologist, occasionally lends a hand in the business. David and his wife, Angela, are also busy raising their two beautiful daughters, Victoria and Juliana. The Preisman family would also like to acknowledge Judith Kiernan, a dear friend and real estate agent with the company for over fifty years.

Today, Preisman Realty is still a successful real estate agency specializing in custom-built homes and sales of existing homes. For more information on Preisman Realty, please call (518) 393-3666, or visit its website at www.preismanrealty.com.

Opposite, top: Ruth and Benjamin Preisman.

Opposite, bottom: Josephine, Ruth, Albert, Sarah, Lillian, and Marcus Friedman.

Above: Richard, Sandra, and Barbara Preisman.

Below: Front row: Juliana and Victoria Preisman. Back row: Angela and David Preisman.

MOHAWK AMBULANCE SERVICE

Established in 1964 with only two vehicles and two employees, Mohawk Ambulance and Oxygen Service operated out of a wash bay of an automotive garage at the corner of State and Brandywine Avenues.

operate the company until 1978 when it was sold to Dr. J. Peter McPartlon, who incorporated it as Parkland Ambulance Service doing business as Mohawk Ambulance Service. Mohawk's first three paramedics were Rich Brandt, Paul Martin, and Jeff Williams, all of whom graduated in 1982 from the REMO Life Support Academy of Albany, New York.

Today, Mohawk Ambulance Service maintains a fleet of thirty ambulances and employs more than 200 people trained to meet medical emergency needs. The service operates from locations in Albany, Schenectady, Troy, and Brunswick. The twenty-four-hour seven-day-week central dispatch center serves the counties of Albany, Schenectady, Troy, and Saratoga.

❖

Above: One of the earlier Mohawk Ambulance vehicles.

Below: The ambulances are shown here outside the Emergency Room of St. Clare's Hospital in Schenectady.

When Mohawk Ambulance and Oxygen Service was founded in 1964 by Ed O'Connor, a Schenectady police officer, its first two employees, Ed Beaupre and Glen Sauter, were paid $1 per call. In 1965, O'Connor sold the business to Fred Fahey, who ran the business until his untimely death in a snowmobiling accident in 1977. Fahey's wife, Barbara, continued to

Mohawk Ambulance moved from 787 State Street to 793 State Street in Schenectady in 1984, the same year the firm purchased and began operating what had been the Schenectady Ambulance Service. The Troy location moved from Oakwood Avenue to 625 River Street in 1985, and Mohawk opened its Albany Station on Quail Street in 1986 and began providing ambulance service in conjunction with

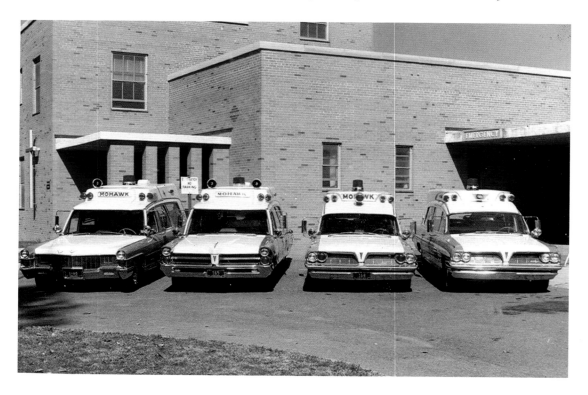

the Albany Fire Department. A second Albany Station and Training Center was opened in 2008 at 570 Central Avenue. The Brunswick location was opened at 42 Brick Church Road in 2002.

Mohawk Ambulance Service is now the largest, privately-owned ambulance service in upstate New York. With thirty ambulances, three fly cars, and two wheelchair vans.

Mohawk provides Basic Life Support and Advanced Life Support services. A state-of-the-art communications center, equipped with a computer-aided dispatch system and GPS tracking system, allows Mohawk to effectively utilize all its resources to provide superior service.

For additional information, please visit www.mohawkambulance.com

❖

Above: A company photo from the 1960s includes Fred Fahey, Bill Frederick, Bill McGroty, Art Parsons, Dan Stec, Eric Olsen, Glen Sauter (one of the original two employees) and William Yamrozy (still employed at Mohawk Ambulance Service).

Below: A Mohawk Ambulance drives around the Saratoga Race Track. Mohawk provides ambulance service at the track.

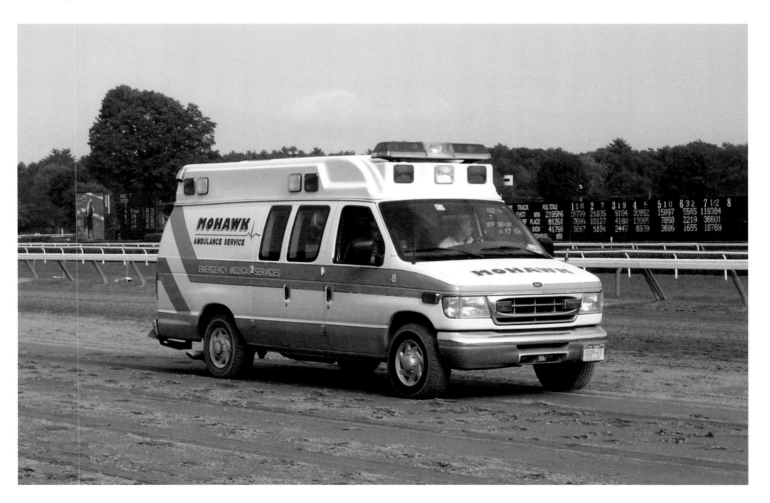

NU-LOOK CAR WASH AND TIRE DISTRIBUTORS

In April 1973, Edward F. "Eddie" Swarczewski and his partner, James Bobar, purchased a local automatic car wash at 1156 Curry Road, Rotterdam, New York. They intended it to be just an investment and kept their full-time jobs. At the time, Edward was employed at Goodyear Tire and Rubber Company as a tire salesman, from which he fondly became known as "Eddie Goodyear" around the local area. So, naturally enough, after he acquired the new business, his customers began referring to him as "Eddie Car Wash." Nu-Look Car Wash started as a car wash only, Edward's investment for his children's college fund. It has become much more.

By July 1975, Edward decided he would go it alone, buying out his partner, quitting his day job, and becoming sole owner. His wife, Theresa, came on board as his accounting manager, and they expanded the business to include wholesale and resale tires, thus changing the name to Nu-Look Car Wash and Tire Sales. Edward was president and treasurer, and Theresa was vice president and secretary.

Kevin, Edward and Theresa's son, got involved in the family business at the beginning of his teenage years. At thirteen he started working part-time for his father, sweeping the parking lot, washing and wiping cars, and anything else his father needed done, including cleaning the bathrooms. Kevin worked part-time for his father through his school years before leaving for college. After his graduation in 1981, Kevin came back to work at Nu-Look. Edward was laying the foundation for Kevin's future, grooming him to take over the family business. By 1982, Kevin had gone full-time and was learning the business inside and out.

❖

Above: Kevin and Edward Swarczewski.

Below: Nu-Look Tire Sales as seen from Curry Road (New York State Route 7).

The tire business continued to exceed their expectations, so much so that in 1984 Edward and Theresa decided to expand, adding an addition to the original building. Kevin's role in the business also grew. In 1985, he became vice president. Edward stayed directly involved in daily operations until his passing on July 28, 2001. With a heavy heart, Kevin became president on August 5, 2001, determined to continue the legacy his father had left. He had been taught that the best attribute of business was good customer service.

Edward loved sales and loved working with the public. He was a people person and customers loved dealing with "Big Ed." Kevin attributes their success to this principle. He believes good customer service embraces many aspects; honesty, fair pricing on good products, understanding the customer's needs and wants, and most of all, treating the customer as a person, not a number. This is what has kept customers coming back to Nu-Look since 1973.

Kevin's father also inspired a sense of loyalty in his employees, some working at the company over sixteen years. One such employee, Nelson Bothmer, has been with them since 1984, starting as a teenager, washing and wiping cars. Today, he is the store manager, and Kevin's right-hand man.

The business continues to grow. Depending on the time of season, Nu-Look employs as many as seven full-time and seven part-time workers. In 2007 a second expansion was begun, construction of a new building behind the existing one. Completed in late 2008, it consists of sixty-six hundred square feet of warehouse space and additional bays for the retail tire business.

Kevin is proud to have continued in his father's footsteps, staying in business and winning the uphill battle against the huge conglomerates. He says it gets tougher every day, but his loyal customers, some from the beginning of Nu-Look Car Wash and Tires, keep him going. His commitment to the success of the business is his way of honoring his late father and company founder, Edward F. "Big Ed" Swarczeski (6/30/1934-7/28/2001).

Above: This 1984 addition is being attached to the rear of the original building.

Below: The lighted Nu-Look sign on a dark December night

TOWN OF NISKAYUNA

The Town of Niskayuna, New York, was established on March 6, 1809, the same day as the County of Schenectady of which it is a part. On that day, its population was 681, but that has now grown to over 22,000. What was once a seventeenth-century hamlet of Niskayuna at the east end of town extended well into what is now the Town of Colonie. In addition to a few older homes built by the Van Vranken family and others that still survive, the town's current 15.1-square-mile area is a mosaic of upscale homes built over the last sixty years. Through its extensive system of parks and natural areas, the town has proudly reserved thirteen percent of its land area that will be forever green.

The town is served by two excellent school systems, that of the Niskayuna Central School District which covers two-thirds of the town and extends into parts of three others, and a part of the South Colonie School District which covers the southeast part of town.

Niskayuna's principal non-residential facilities include GE Global Research, the Knolls Atomic Power Laboratory, the Bellevue Woman's Care Hospital, Environment One, the laboratory of the SI Group, television station WRGB, and Mohawk Commons shopping center.

Niskayuna and the adjacent Town of Glenville with whom we share this page comprise the Third District of Schenectady County and together elect five of its fifteen legislators. Through jointly sponsored activities throughout the year, the Niskayuna Town Board is proud to join with the Schenectady County Legislature to celebrate this bicentennial year of 2009.

TOWN OF GLENVILLE

The Town of Glenville, New York, incorporated in 1821, is a town of geographic diversity; from riverfront to wooded hills to quiet, suburban neighborhoods, to bustling business corridors, Glenville has a place for every taste. This beautiful town is replete with nature preserves, traditional and riverfront parks, some of the best fishing holes along the Mohawk River, and a rich history that includes the colonial period and the industrial revolution. One such historic landmark is the Green's Corners One-Room Schoolhouse, built in 1825.

The Empire State Aerosciences Museum on Saratoga Road in Glenville is the place to view the past and present of New York State's contribution to aviation.

Wolf Hollow Gorge, a natural wonder fashioned by a geological fault, displays one hundred foot cliffs and many plant species native only to this area.

The town also boasts a thriving riverfront, featuring three restaurant/ banquet houses and regular special events during the summer months.

While in Upstate New York, stop in and experience the sights and sounds that are Glenville. In the meantime, for more information please visit www.townofglenville.org.

INDEX

SPONSORS

ABOUT THE AUTHOR

BILL BUELL

William H. "Bill" Buell is a journalist for the *Daily Gazette* newspaper of Schenectady, New York. He is a reporter and writer whose duties encompass feature stories that center on local and New York State history, cultural and theatrical events, and profiles of the persons involved in these areas of interest. He is also responsible for two monthly features called "Landmarks" and "Focus on Faith." Prior to his current assignments, he was a sportswriter and columnist for the *Gazette*, work for which he received numerous awards. Bill holds the B.A. in history from the University at Albany and is an active member and volunteer of the Schenectady County Historical Society.

ABOUT THE EDITOR

EDWIN D. REILLY, JR.

Edwin D. Reilly, Jr., president of the Schenectady County Historical Society, is also a trustee of the Schenectady County Public Library, a consultant to the Edison Exploratorium in Schenectady, archivist for the Schenectady Torch Club, and a regular contributor to the opinion pages of Schenectady's *Sunday Gazette*. Previously, he had served nine two-year terms as supervisor of the Schenectady County town of Niskayuna. Dr. Reilly, who holds the Ph.D. in physics from Rensselaer Polytechnic Institute, is emeritus professor of computer science at the State University of New York at Albany and is the author or editor of several books on the history of computing and information technology and two on historical topics pertaining to his town.

ABOUT THE COVER

L. F. TANTILLO

Len Tantillo was born and raised in upstate New York, and attended Rhode Island School of Design. From 1969 to 1976 he worked as an architectural designer and acquired a working knowledge of building design and construction. During his apprenticeship the focus of his work shifted to visual presentation and in 1976 he began working as a free-lance architectural illustrator. In 1980, Tantillo was commissioned to depict a series of nineteenth-century structures from archeological artifacts and historic documents. Similar projects followed, many of which were located along the banks of the Hudson River near Albany, New York. In 1984, Tantillo left commercial art and began the full-time pursuit of fine art. He has spent the last twenty-five years creating numerous historical and marine paintings, which have continued to draw a wide audience. Tantillo's studio is located in southern Rensselaer County, New York.

For more information, please visit www.lftantillo.com.

For more information about the following publications or about publishing your own book, please call
Historical Publishing Network at 800-749-9790 or visit www.lammertinc.com.

Black Gold: The Story of Texas Oil & Gas

Garland: A Contemporary History

Historic Abilene: An Illustrated History

Historic Alamance County: An Illustrated History

Historic Albuquerque: An Illustrated History

Historic Amarillo: An Illustrated History

Historic Anchorage: An Illustrated History

Historic Austin: An Illustrated History

Historic Baldwin County: A Bicentennial History

Historic Baton Rouge: An Illustrated History

Historic Beaufort County: An Illustrated History

Historic Beaumont: An Illustrated History

Historic Bexar County: An Illustrated History

Historic Birmingham: An Illustrated History

Historic Brazoria County: An Illustrated History

Historic Charlotte:
An Illustrated History of Charlotte and Mecklenburg County

Historic Cheyenne: A History of the Magic City

Historic Comal County: An Illustrated History

Historic Corpus Christi: An Illustrated History

Historic DeKalb County: An Illustrated History

Historic Denton County: An Illustrated History

Historic Edmond: An Illustrated History

Historic El Paso: An Illustrated History

Historic Erie County: An Illustrated History

Historic Fairbanks: An Illustrated History

Historic Gainesville & Hall County: An Illustrated History

Historic Gregg County: An Illustrated History

Historic Hampton Roads: Where America Began

Historic Hancock County: An Illustrated History

Historic Henry County: An Illustrated History

Historic Houston: An Illustrated History

Historic Illinois: An Illustrated History

Historic Kern County:
An Illustrated History of Bakersfield and Kern County

Historic Lafayette:
An Illustrated History of Lafayette & Lafayette Parish

Historic Laredo:
An Illustrated History of Laredo & Webb County

Historic Lee County: The Story of Fort Myers & Lee County

Historic Louisiana: An Illustrated History

Historic Midland: An Illustrated History

Historic Montgomery County:
An Illustrated History of Montgomery County, Texas

Historic Ocala: The Story of Ocala & Marion County

Historic Oklahoma: An Illustrated History

Historic Oklahoma County: An Illustrated History

Historic Omaha:
An Illustrated History of Omaha and Douglas County

Historic Orange County: An Illustrated History

Historic Ouachita Parish: An Illustrated History

Historic Paris and Lamar County: An Illustrated History

Historic Pasadena: An Illustrated History

Historic Passaic County: An Illustrated History

Historic Pennsylvania An Illustrated History

Historic Philadelphia: An Illustrated History

Historic Prescott:
An Illustrated History of Prescott & Yavapai County

Historic Richardson: An Illustrated History

Historic Rio Grande Valley: An Illustrated History

Historic Scottsdale: A Life from the Land

Historic Shelby County: An Illustrated History

Historic Shreveport-Bossier:
An Illustrated History of Shreveport & Bossier City

Historic South Carolina: An Illustrated History

Historic Smith County: An Illustrated History

Historic Temple: An Illustrated History

Historic Texas: An Illustrated History

Historic Victoria: An Illustrated History

Historic Tulsa: An Illustrated History

Historic Williamson County: An Illustrated History

Historic Wilmington & The Lower Cape Fear:
An Illustrated History

Historic York County: An Illustrated History

Iron, Wood & Water: An Illustrated History of Lake Oswego

Jefferson Parish: Rich Heritage, Promising Future

Miami's Historic Neighborhoods: A History of Community

Old Orange County Courthouse: A Centennial History

Plano: An Illustrated Chronicle

The New Frontier:
A Contemporary History of Fort Worth & Tarrant County

The San Gabriel Valley: A 21st Century Portrait

The Spirit of Collin County

Valley Places, Valley Faces

Water, Rails & Oil: Historic Mid & South Jefferson County